ENABLED by PARDON

TO HEAR THE VOICE
OF SILENCE

HENRY OEGEMA

ENABLED
by
PARDON

TO HEAR THE VOICE
OF SILENCE

Tate Publishing & Enterprises

 TATE PUBLISHING
& Enterprises

Book design copyright © 2007 by Tate Publishing, LLC. All rights reserved.
Cover design by Elizabeth Mason
Interior design by Janae Glass

Published in the United States of America

ISBN: 1–5988664–5-1
06.11.09

Acknowledgements

I believe it is fitting to acknowledge that some people have put a great deal of their time over the years into helping me get this into print. One of these is my friend Mark Dribnenky, who would edit and type all my hand-written notes into very neatly formatted handouts for Sunday school classes.

Then years later, when I had taken all my notes and expanded on them so they were in a more readable format, my nephew Jeremy took all this information and put it into his computer and handed me a CD.

Never having had any interest in computers and not knowing anything about how to use one, I was persuaded by friends to get a laptop and shown how to use it a little so I could make some changes or additions to the text.

I want to acknowledge my parents, who have both passed into eternity, for a home where the peace of God was an unconscious and established blessing, where humility was abundantly displayed and self–sacrifice was normal.

It is there that I learned by observation that, even though God doesn't say much audibly, He says what He means and means what He says. And He did put it in writing.

I am grateful that He has left us His Spirit of truth. For as Jesus said in John 16:14 "He shall glorify Me; for He shall take of Mine, and shall disclose it to you."

This He has done over the centuries through nature, His Word, and His people, many of whom have left a written text for others to benefit from.

A few books among the many others over the years of my

life have been a great resource for me and very helpful in appreciating and understanding the tabernacle and its offerings. They are: *Gleanings in Exodus* by Arthur W. Pink, published by Moody Press (quotations and references have been used by permission and with my appreciation); *Leviticus* by Andrew Bonar, published by Banner of Truth (quotations and references have been used with permission and with my appreciation; and finally, *The Holy Vessels and Furniture of the Tabernacle* by Henry Soltau, published by Kreger Publications.

Table of Contents

Introduction

I was born with an appetite for wanting to know how things work. Many will just drive a car, but I want to know what makes it go. I am of the technical sort. Where most people are content to sit in an airplane and let the pilot fly it, I look at the wings and engines, thinking about the air flowing over and under the wings and through the engines and about the delicate balance between lift and weight, thrust and drag. There is the remarkable reliability of compression, ignition, combustion and expansion of air. These things all work because there is a God who spoke and continues to speak unfailing reliability into a universe.

My appetite for wanting to know how things work has also affected my interest in God's revealed and unfailing order by which we can approach and know Him. This can be understood in part from the physical realm that He spoke into existence. But we can more specifically understand this from the examples and illustrations and teaching in the scriptures. And to assist in understanding these, He has provided His Spirit, by which He draws us to convict and reveal this unfailing order of God. What the Spirit reveals, the eyes have not seen nor has the mind understood, but is received by faith and believed.

Psalm 19, in its opening statement declares:

> The heavens are telling of the glory of God, and their expanse is declaring the work of His hands. Day to day pours forth speech, and night to night reveals knowledge. There is no speech, nor are there words. Their voice is not heard. Their line has gone out through all the earth and their utterance to the end of the world.

So the created order has a message, and it can be seen, it speaks without words, declares the work of His hands, pours forth speech, and reveals knowledge.

The scriptures do not speak audibly, either. They also silently declare. Just as creation must be observed, so the scriptures must be read and meditated upon. The Spirit of God then reveals what cannot be seen, namely its intended instruction and purpose.

In it is described a three dimensional image of the heavenly tabernacle, made of created things and its meaning to be revealed by the Spirit. It tells and declares and pours forth speech and reveals knowledge without making a sound. Inside the holy place, there was a scene of divine glory. Gold covered the walls, pillars, table of bread and altar of incense. The lampstand and mercy seat were pure hammered gold. This is where silence reigned. Here, the voice of man was still, but the vessels spoke. Silently they told of the glories of Christ: the redeemer of man, the keeper of the law, the example of a king who lived as a servant.

He was the Father's delight and spoke with the authority of God. He radiated the glories of heaven to a world living in darkness. He could intercede from the depth of holy perfection—with brokenness of heart for the helpless condition of His creation. And with the humility of the love of God, He did not insist on His rights as God, but died as a criminal, was resurrected and raised to glory.

Why look at this tabernacle which was an image of things to come when the Christ it portrayed has already come? Why listen to these silent components of a tabernacle? We might also ask if any other portions of the Bible speak with an audible voice. Does the Holy Spirit speak with an audible voice? Does He not take of what Jesus is and quietly reveal Him to those who seek and trust Him? Should we not first learn to be impressed by Him before we go expressing ourselves about Him?

Long before the tabernacle of David—who introduced a new form of worship foreshadowing the age of the church to come— was there not this tabernacle of Moses where Israel had to learn how to listen to God? Is a transformed mind not essential to prevent human emotion and sentiment to be mistaken for the Holy Spirit? Has the Holy Spirit not always been trying to reveal the person of Christ to the world and to the people of God?

How remarkable is the gift of faith He brings! With it we can see and experience the horrors of sin and, in contrast to it, the abundance of grace and mercy. There are many examples where one person could see or understand what another could not. Think of what Abel could see in the lamb and Cain could not. What Jacob could see in the birthright and Esau could not. Joseph saw dreams his brothers did not. David saw his inheritance of kingship while Saul saw only his gift. The prophets saw the future while Israel saw the present. Nebuchadnezzar could only see the dreams while Daniel could see interpretation. Stephen could see the heavens opened while the Jerusalem council could only see their traditions and the power to control them. Saul saw the power of grace and Agrippa the power of his throne. Mary could see in Jesus what Judas could not. She could see the coming and final sacrifice Jesus would offer to fulfill everything that had been foreshadowed for 1400 years. Jesus acknowledged that her act and gift were in preparation for this event, and she would be remembered throughout history for it. Everywhere on the pages of scripture, the one could see what the other could not.

Moses, the humblest man on earth, could see God and go into the tent of the presence. David, with a heart after God, could go in and sit before God. Stephen, full of the Holy Spirit, could see the heavens opened. Saul, a chosen instrument, was caught up into the third heaven. Peter had a vision of the clean and the unclean. John had a vision of things to come.

These people had encounters and enduring relationships with God, which confirms that they not only had access into the presence of God, but they lived a life that made that access unhindered. What is necessary for such access, the tabernacle illustrates in detail.

In contrast, we now find our culture leaving its mark on our minds and thoughts. We live in a world of supermarkets, shopping plazas and smorgasbords from which we select as much or as little of everything that is offered in colorful, attractive and convenient sized packages.

We also prefer God to be of the variety we like. How often He does not meet our expectations based on our sin-created needs.

To the extent we adopt our cultural thinking, we will be faced with a corresponding skepticism. Once we form God in our imagination to be in our image, we then also reject Jesus the Christ, who " . . . is the image of the invisible God (Col. 1:15)." We then prefer the promises of God without the problems associated with them; a Daniel without a lion's den, a Paul without a prison, a church without persecution. We will prefer a user-friendly ecumenism to a sword that cuts bone from marrow. We will emphasize a single phrase or text out of an entire passage, psalm or hymn—a church not unlike the religious order of Jesus' day. They could celebrate the great feast of tabernacles and not recognize the Jesus it pointed to standing in their midst.

Jesus had only His Father's word. But that made His testimony a sharp, two-edged sword. It cut through the powers of darkness and sin to set its prisoners free. He did not attempt to bypass humiliation so He could put on His crown in the holy of holies. Isaiah foresaw this some seven hundred years before and prophesied it of Jesus, in Isa. 50:7: "Therefore I have set my face like flint, and I know that I will not be ashamed."

This may not be a popular thought today, but it is a necessary one. Without this ingredient, there would be no redemption. He was not afraid to address the sins of pride, legalism and hypocrisy, yet He could demonstrate endless compassion for the poor, the needy and the outcasts.

No one ever lived a more normal Christian life and affected the human race more than Jesus did. He demonstrated the most balanced life, composed of every necessary ingredient. The temple and tabernacle had illustrated these for fourteen hundred years. Yet even with these examples before us, we still see dimly through a dark glass.

We prefer to *think with our feelings* and *listen with our eyes.* But faith comes by *hearing with our ears.* If all the great wisdom of the world is foolishness to God, then a renewed mind is required to think the thoughts of God and to stand in His presence. We would do well to fill ourselves with the fullness He revealed of Himself.

God knows we are quite accustomed to living in darkness. He even says we love the darkness. But we can also be filled with light, or every shade of gray in between. In Hebrews alone, we read of six different hearts. Hebrews chapter 3 mentions *three* kinds: the hardened heart (verse 8), the erring heart (verse 10), and the evil heart of unbelief (verse 12). The natural mind prefers and finds these easy to live with. They are close relatives of the three soils in Luke 8:5, and represents the portion of our present generation that gets most of all the media attention. These have demonstrated they love the darkness.

Three more different hearts are in the second half of Hebrews. There is a heart in which God's law is written (Heb.8:10), a true heart sprinkled with blood (Heb.10:22), and a heart established by grace (Heb.13:9). These are like the fourth seed of Luke 8, demonstrating a passion and love for the truth about self and God.

It is between the first and second three that we find Heb. 4:12.

> For the word of God is living and active and sharper than any
> two-edged sword, and piercing as far as the division of soul and
> spirit, of both joints and marrow, and able to judge the thoughts
> and intentions of the heart.

This word, in history past and present was spoken by ordinary men and women, by prophets, kings and priests were inspired by the Spirit and empowered by God to change hearts and embrace His fullness. As ignorance of this witness increases in society and church, they become progressively more selective of what they choose to believe or reject, like the first three hearts.

Wheat and tares will continue to grow side by side. It's the ratio that concerns me. I am confident the remedy to reverse the invasion of culture into the church will be far less popular than the best-selling and most read books of our day, and therefore discarded by most.

Not unlike ancient past and present day Israel, I sadly see that my country and the church within it does not avail itself of the opportunity to hold fast what God has entrusted to it. It has cast away its unprecedented access to the Word and God who wrote it and rapidly sinks deeper into a spiritual darkness without foundations.

The dark ages before the Reformation were not a result of a lack of song and music, but a problem of theology. The reformers restored a new obedience to the Word, after the example of Jesus, who said in John 8:28 "I do nothing on my own initiative, but I speak these things as the Father taught Me."

John, in 1:14, testifies that " . . . the Word became flesh and *dwelt* among us." This word *"dwelt"* means to tent or encamp or reside as God did in the tabernacle of old. So we can say Jesus "tabernacled" among us.

Moses constructed the tabernacle in the same manner of obedience. And Paul speaks of New Testament believers as being "tabernacles" (II Pet.1:13; I Cor. 3:16). It would therefore be helpful to know what the tabernacle structure and its contents have to teach us about being tabernacles.

I admit to knowing more about the tabernacle than is realized in my life. Death, pain, suffering, rejection, humiliation, ridicule, etc. are not at the top of my list of preferences. It has always been easier to use the gifts of God to impress others than for Jesus to become realized as an unconscious manifestation in our lives. There has not been a single point in all the places of the tabernacle where I have not seen my own failure in life to apprehend what the type reveals of the life of Jesus. And this not only of the physical Jesus we see in the outer court, but even more so of the resurrected Jesus we see portrayed in the holy place. This does have the great benefit of bringing to mind and heart all that Jesus availed for us. These–His own perfections–He is now presenting before the Father as an advocate on our behalf.

I am grateful for all the teaching and writing of others that have affected my life. I have not meant to just copy or repeat what someone else said or wrote, though there is probably little that has not been influenced by them over the years of my life. It's for this reason that I understand there are parents and children, teachers and students. Truth, faith, understanding and information are meant to be passed on from one to another. To the question "what is truth?" that Pilate puts to Jesus, John records twenty-two references Jesus had spoken in answer. Pilate had not been listening.

I am sorry that understanding the tabernacle was not impressed upon me earlier in my life, and I find it to be a very neglected part of God's word. There is great value in knowing how Jesus was illustrated in the tabernacle. It sets forth a very succinct and complete picture of the work of Christ Jesus that satisfied the Father on our behalf, and is an excellent foundation on which to understand New Testament teaching. It is also a great tool by which to examine one's own journey into the fullness of Christ. What has been put on? What is missing? What is overemphasized? Why is it not working in one's life? It is *like a map* with directions that tells you if you're *going east* towards the gate and from the place of God's presence or you're *going west* toward the holy place and nearer His presence.

Every chapter I have purposely kept brief. One can choose to read them in any order. I did not mean this to be a commentary nor a novel. It won't be an easy read. No one comprehends the tabernacle in one evening. Moses received his instruction over 40 days and comprehended far more than me, even though my interest has not diminished in ten years. Be prepared to take the necessary time to think about its order and content. The layout as it was given by God to Moses was not to satisfy our personal preference or convenience.

I begin with some 40 pages of background from the first four books of Moses and the sin problem for which the human race has no solution, other than the one provided by God Himself and placed in the midst of His people. Entrance is then made through the gate into the provision of God's redemption going west toward the Ark of the Covenant.

While the ark points to our future glorification, the altar of incense is the destination in our present life. There, with all its privileges and responsibilities as a holy, royal priesthood, we have access to all the fullness of Christ. The Father waits and jealously desires for His redeemed to come as a people of depth and humility, broken of pride and dead to sin, to take their place as a royal priesthood of intercessors on behalf of a fallen world before Him. Welcome on this journey of truth revealed from ages past.

Can Two Walk Together

Amos 3:3

Unless They Be Agreed?

Into the formless void and darkness of planet earth entered the Spirit of God to speak into existence a likeness of His own light and endless variety of life. The responsibility of developing and maintaining this earth He assigned to man—the likeness He had made of Himself.

There was good reason, then, for man to walk in agreement with God. But a day came when God came searching for Adam, while Adam had chosen to hide himself from God.

Since that day, fellowship with God has not been one of man's highest priorities, even though God's desire for this fellowship has moved him constantly nearer to the heart of fallen man.

From this early beginning, God promised to crush Satan's head, He walked with Enoch, saved Noah's family during the flood, called Abram from Ur, and from his descendants established an entire nation. Through them He chose to reveal Himself to the world and bless it.

His desire was greater than just to direct them with laws and regulations. He wanted to *"dwell among them"* (Ex. 25:8). The Hebrew word for neighbor is closely related to this. *"There I will meet with you"* (Ex. 25:22). was his promise. Moses did not decide to build this sanctuary and then invite God to it.

From 1441–965 BC, (476 years) the tabernacle functioned for Israel. They went from slavery to possession of their land, from wandering in a wilderness to settlement, from tents to houses.

From 965–586 BC, Solomon's temple stood for 379 years, during which time God's promise of Ex. 23:31 was realized.

From 586–515 BC, Judah, following Israel's example 137 years before, went into captivity, and there:"By the rivers of Babylon, there we sat down and wept" (Ps.137:1). It was not the first time they had failed to walk with God.

From 515–20 BC, the reconstructed temple stood for 495 years. It appeared as nothing compared to the former temple (Ezra 3:12, Hag. 2:3).

During the first half of the next 88 years, this temple was enlarged by Herod and his successors, and stood until its fall in 68 AD. During that time, Jesus often visited the outer courts, called *hieron* in Greek.

The Greek word *naos* referred to the smaller inner sanctuary portion, where similar furniture and ministries of the ancient tabernacle were found.

The English Bible uses the word temple for both naos and hieron. But it was in the naos that the typology of Jesus was represented.

In John 2:15 Jesus drives the temple merchants out of *the hieron*. In verse 21, He equates the *naos with himself*. This distinction is important.

In the book of Acts, which gives mainly a *historical account*, the word hieron is used 25 times because it gives a location for what was happening. There are two places where the plural for naos is used referring to God not living in temples made with human hands (Acts 7:48, 17:24).

From Romans to Revelations, which are mainly *teaching books*, only the word *naos* is used, with one exception in I Cor 9:13 that refers to the priests receiving food offerings in the outer court as their pay.

So when Paul wrote to the Corinthians, he used the word *naos* for the word *temple*."Do you not know that you are a temple of God and that the Spirit of God dwells in you? If any man destroys the temple of God, God will destroy him" (I Cor. 3:16,17). God had moved from visiting and dwelling *with* man, to dwelling *among* them, to now dwelling *in* them.

Though the law did not allow Jesus beyond the altar and into the naos, there was no law to prevent Jesus from coming out of the naos. All that was represented in type in the naos, now walked in the midst of Israel, and very few realized it. By many incurable shoppers, He was despised and rejected.

At His glorious transfiguration on the mountain, Jesus himself showed the effect of a life lived in the naos (Mark 9:2).

When Paul writes to the Romans that they should "be transformed by the renewing of the mind" in Rom. 12:2, the Greek word he uses is *metamorphose*, the same word used of Jesus at his transfiguration. In other words, *be transfigured*. God was sparing nothing in order to once again restore man into a place of union and agreement with himself.

Jesus saying, "Therefore you are to be perfect, as your heavenly Father is perfect" (Matt. 5:48), is not unlike Paul saying "be transformed" (Rom. 12:2,) or "that you may be filled up to all the fullness of God (Eph. 3:19)." And then he adds in the next chapter, "to the measure of the stature which belongs to the fullness of Christ (Eph. 4:13)." And to the Colossians he writes, "To whom God willed to make known what is the riches of the glory of this mystery among the gentiles, which is Christ in you, the hope of glory" (Col. 1:27).

His desire is to finish the work He began. "He who began a good work in you will perfect it until the day of Jesus Christ" (Phil. 1:6).

It was the prayer of Jesus for His people.

> "I do not pray for these alone, but also for those who will believe in me through their word; that they may all be one, as You Father, are in Me, and I in You, that they also may

be one in Us, that the world may believe that You sent Me. And the glory which You gave Me, I have given to them, that they may be one, just as We are one; I in them and You in Me, that they may be made perfect in one , . . . Father I desire that they also whom You gave Me, may be with Me where I am, that they may behold My glory which You have given Me;"–John 17:20–24 (NKJV)

If the Son Sets You Free

John 8:36

Freedom in God's Design

In Luke 2:1 we read, "a decree went out from Caesar Augustus that a census be taken, so the entire world should be taxed." In Luke 2:6 we read that the day arrived for Mary to give birth.

While Caesar ruled and taxed and ordered and lorded over his domain, Mary, the bond slave of the Lord, humbly gave the world its greatest servant. *In humility lies a wealth of freedom to serve.*

The contrast between the reign of Christ and the Anti-Christ is huge. As Jesus said,

> "You know that the rulers of the Gentiles lord it over them and their great men exercise authority over them. It is not so among you, but whoever wishes to become great among you shall be your servant, and whoever wishes to be the first among you shall be your slave."–Matt. 20:25–26

After a summary of the covenant had been given in Ex. 20–23 and ratified in Ex. 24, we find Moses on the mountain receiving instruction in Ex. 25.

> "Tell the sons of Israel to raise a contribution for Me,"–verse 2

God was telling Israel to bring an offering to construct His dwelling place, so

> "... that I may dwell among them."–verse 8

God was looking to dwell among a people of servant hearts.

The Redeemer Himself, as leader and servant of Israel, was fulfilling the song that Moses and Israel had sung after crossing the sea,

> "The Lord is my strength and song. He has become my salvation. He is my God, and I will prepare Him a habitation"–*Ex. 15:2*.

Israel was set free from Egypt to delight themselves in the presence of God among them. In trusting dependence they would receive far more of Him than their grumbling ever did.

Though there was already a "tent of meeting" (Ex 33:7), before the tabernacle was constructed, the tabernacle became a more abundant revelation of Christ in their midst feeding and guiding them.

They were already aware of the Sabbath law in Ex 16:23–30 when manna was provided. They were already familiar with sacrifices and offerings from the days of their forefathers" (Gen 8:20; 22:2).

They could have said, "We already know enough." Instead they made the tabernacle with willing hands and of available material.

To all who freely came to work, God gave skill to "make all that I have commanded you" (Ex 31:6). God filled Bezalel and Oholiab "with the spirit of God in wisdom, in understanding, in knowledge, and in all kinds of craftsmanship" (Ex. 31:3). Just as now in the church there are varieties of gifts, ministries and effects (I Cor. 12).

God "works all things after the council of His will" (Eph. 1:11). He is a free and self-determining being who acts according to His own perfections.

We were created in that image as beings possessing the moral freedom to make our own choices of obedience or rebellion.

Though God has the ability to intervene and often does, He frequently does not. This leaves us to see in time the consequences of our actions. He does visit our iniquity (perverted truth or sin that I am content to live with) upon us and our descendents for three or four generations (Ex. 20:5).

Since the day of Adam's choice, we have all been bent on following his example. His first choice to disobey was followed by a second choice to suppress the truth and blame someone else. He chose to become willfully ignorant of the responsibility God gave him.

This is quite well stated in Pauls' letter to the Romans in 1:18–23.

> "For the wrath of God is revealed from heaven against all ungodliness and unrighteousness of men, who suppress the truth in unrighteousness, because that which is known about God is evident within them; for God made it evident to them.
>
> For since the creation of the world His invisible attributes, His eternal power and divine nature, have been clearly seen, being understood through what has been made, so that they are without excuse. For even though they knew God, they did not honor Him as God, or give thanks; . . . Professing to be wise they became fools."

There is no freedom in deception nor in the suppression of truth.

In Ex. 40:33, Moses and Israel have finished the work, and God's presence moves in. Nothing was left to the imagination of Moses.

Jesus, in His own ministry, taught, "freely you have received, freely give" (Matt. .10:8). He who spoke words of healing, multiplied bread and did everything according to what the Father said (John 5:19; 8:26) concluded His ministry by saying, "It is finished" (John 19:30).

Paul could say, "I have finished my course" (II Tim. 4:7).

The seventh angel will blow the last trumpet, and "the mystery of God should be finished" (Rev. 10:7).

Others need to be encouraged. "Take heed to the ministry which you have received in the Lord that you may fulfill it" (Col. 4:17).

The tabernacle was finished when it was built according to the pattern God had shown Moses" (Ex. 25:9, 40; 26:30). It was a copy of things in the heavens (Heb. 9:23). We, also, as tabernacles, will be finished when we are according to the likeness of Christ. The "It is finished" must be of the Father's design or freedom will perish.

God desired Israel to comprehend the breadth and length and height and depth and love of Christ, which surpasses knowledge, that they would desire to, "be filled up to all the fullness of God" (Eph. 3:19). That is freedom!

A Long Story!

Luke 24:27, 44

What Did He Say?

On the road to Emmaus, we find Jesus explaining the things concerning Himself in all the scriptures, beginning with Moses and the prophets and the Psalms. On that journey, Jesus did what the Holy Spirit would continue to do for us after He left.

Perhaps He began by describing the things that He had spoken into existence at the creation and reminded them of the 19th Psalm.

"The heavens are telling of the glory of God, and their expanse is declaring the work of His hand. Day to day pours forth speech, and night to night reveals knowledge."

He may have explained how He was "the seed of the woman" and represented in Enoch, Noah, Melchizidek, Abram, Joseph and Moses. How He was the Passover Lamb, the Smitten Rock, the Kinsman Redeemer, Son of David, Wisdom of God, Suffering Servant, Glory of God, Coming Messiah, Hope of Israel, Desire of the Nations, Righteous Branch, to name a few.

He may have illustrated Himself in different ministries:

In Genesis *as our calling*, choosing out of Adam's race a people like Noah, Job and Abraham to live by faith in Him.

In Exodus *as our sanctuary*, detailing in the tabernacle His fullness and provision for restored nearness.

In Leviticus *as our sacrifice* by illustrating in the offerings, sacrifices and feasts how all of ones needs are met for complete redemption.

In Numbers *as our guide* by directing the ordering of Israel and going before them in the cloud during the years of the wilderness journey.

In Deuteronomy *as our sanctifier*, reminding, warning and preparing His people to live in the provisions promised to their forefather Abraham.

He may have mentioned how He had magnified *the law of the Lord* (it controls our conduct), which is perfect, restoring the soul.

How *the testimony of the Lord* (explaining who He is) is sure, making wise the simple.

How the *precepts of the Lord* (rules for action) or statutes (legislative enactments) are right, making the heart rejoice because they are principles for living, trusting, giving and serving.

How *the commandments of the Lord* (specific instructions) are pure and enlighten the eyes. They are binding and will never change.

How *the fear of the Lord* is clean and endures forever, instructing us in the worship of obedience and extravagant love.

How the *judgments of the Lord* are true and righteous and they can be trusted. They are verdicts on the destiny of man.

He may have told them how He was in Psalm 23, where "the Lord is my shepherd"–*Raah* (my shepherd). "I shall not want"–*Jireh* (my provider). "He leads me beside quiet waters"–*Shalom* (my peace). "He restores my soul"–*Rophi* (my healer). "He guides me in the path of righteousness"–*Tsidkenu* (my righteousness). "I fear no evil for you are with me"–*Shammah* (my God who is there). "You have anointed my head"–*Nissi* (My banner over me).

He may have told the disciples of the seven fold Spirit of God mentioned in Isaiah 11:2 and the "I am's" He had spoken of to them in His own lifetime. He may have illustrated how they were present in the tabernacle and temple.

How at the Gate, *The Spirit of Wisdom* revealed the "*I am the door*" that would draw people to repentance, believing His foolishness to be wiser than the world's wisdom.

How at the Altar, *The Spirit of Understanding* revealed the "*I am the good shepherd who lays down His life for the sheep*" to convince man of the completeness of his redemption and bring the understanding that it was all of grace and not works.

How at the Laver, *The Spirit of Counsel* revealed the "*I am the way, the truth and the life*" to teach (council) the importance of sanctification by the washing of water (with the Word).

How at the Table, *The Spirit of Strength* revealed the "*I am the bread of life*" to feed us with the love and delight of the Father and strengthen us with covenant union.

How at the Lampstand, *The Spirit of Knowledge* revealed the "*I am the light of the world*" who fills with the knowledge of Christ to equip us with love and compassion for the world that needs to know the fullness of Christ and Christ crucified.

How at the Altar of Incense, *The Spirit of the Fear of the Lord* revealed the "*I am the resurrection*" who with brokenness acknowledges the need of man; and with depth of compassion appeals to the character of God; and with humility understands we have no merit of our own, as He intercedes for us with the Father.

How at the Ark of the Covenant, *the Spirit of the Lord* revealed the "*I am that I am*" who as the author, keeper and guardian of the law, would restore all things unto the Father in perfect union.

He may have concluded the *Spirit of Truth* would come and "He shall take of Mine and shall disclose it to you" (John 16:14). He would guide into all truth, discern errors, expose hidden faults, reveal presumptuous sin, free those who were under the dominion of sin, and acquit people of great transgressions so that the meditations of the heart would be acceptable in His sight.

He Speaks to Instruct
II Tim. 3:16
His Authority to Teach

Genesis, the book of beginnings, covers some three thousand years, perhaps four or five thousand years. Exodus covers no more than 82 years.

The first two and a half chapters of Exodus take us through some 40 years of Moses' life. His next 40 years are covered in only 15 verses. Chapters 3–40 is one year and begins the third 40–year period of Moses' life, during which he is called to lead Israel to their promised land.

Here God begins to establish Israel as a nation. They accept the law, ratify the covenant agreement, and receive the grace to enjoy Him forever. While very little detail is given about the ark of Noah, a great amount of instruction is given for the tabernacle.

In times past, God has introduced Himself by various names:

Elohim	*Gen. 1:1: God of strength, mighty leader and supreme deity.*
El Elyon	*Gen. 14:22: God most high and sovereign.*
El Olam	*Gen 21:33: God of eternity, everlasting God.*
El Shaddai	*Gen 17:1: the almighty one.*
Yahweh	*Gen. 2:4: I am the one who is, the self-existent one, and Israel's redeemer. It is associated with God's holiness and hatred for sin.*
Yahweh Yireh	*Gen. 22:14: The Lord will see to it (my provider).*
Yahweh Nissi	*Ex. 17:15: the Lord is my banner over me.*

In time, Yahweh was substituted with Adonai (Lord or Master, who purposes to bless), by those who feared mispronouncing or using God's name in vain.

In Ex. 6:3, El Shaddai was about to introduce Himself to Egypt through Moses and the ten plagues.

In Ex. 6:6, He is to be presented to Israel as Kinsmen Redeemer (*Go'el* in Hebrew), one who has a close personal relationship with the redeemed.

After 430 years of living under the promises of God Most High (El Elyon) to Abraham in Gen. 13:14–18, Israel might have been excited about leaving Egypt. With the wealth of Egypt handed to them, they are driven out of Egypt (Ex. 12:40,41), cry to Moses for fear of their lives on one side of the sea, and sing the song of Moses for a great deliverance on the other.

Considering the obvious involvement of God in the Exodus, Israel did not appear to be excited about life lived by faith in the foolishness of God's wisdom and ways. But then neither is our generation.

On the journey through the Sinai, they murmur, complain and grumble over water and food, which God abundantly provides.

Having arrived at Horeb, the mountain of God (Ex. 3:1,12) chapters 20–23 give a brief summary of a three-fold law, which was *a revelation of holiness.*

The *moral law* controlled individual life. It made nothing perfect. It could not save. It demanded life, but could not give it. It restrained people, but could not inspire them. The *civil law* governed national life. The *ceremonial law* governed religious life.

In chapter 24, seventy elders of Israel and God ratify this covenant by eating a meal in the presence of God on the mountain.

Having placed Israel under holy perfection and thereby condemnation, He proceeds to provide for Israel, in chapters 25–

40, *the way to holiness* in the tabernacle. In providing the means of grace for Israel to come to Him, God is giving Israel what they *did not deserve*. (In the offerings and sacrifices of Leviticus, we see God's mercy, not giving Israel what they *did deserve)*.

We see everywhere in the dimensions and quantities the multiple of *five*, which is the number that represents *grace*.

	The dimensions	The quantities
Holy of holies	10x10x10	100 silver sockets
The holy place	20x10x10	15 bars 10 curtains
The tabernacle	30x10x10	200 loops 100 clasps
The court	100x50x 5	60 poles 60 sockets
The gate	20x5	
The door	10x10	5 pillars
The veil	10x10	5 animals
The bronze altar	5x5x5	5 offerings

God alone could direct the construction and purpose of the tabernacle. As He so commonly does, here also He speaks to instruct by arranging the components (furniture) in the form of a cross, long before the Romans used them for their own purposes of subjecting people under their rule.

The journey from the gate to the ark was narrow. It brought death to every carnal idea anyone may have had of God or how to approach Him. Though it was narrow, it was as wide as His outstretched crucified arms. His invitation was, "For whoever will call upon the name of the Lord will be saved" (Rom 10:13).

He chose to use man and what was available to man to construct His dwelling place. God will never ask from man what has not already been given to him. In the finished tabernacle, everything pointed in type to the complete work of Israel's coming Redeemer.

Paul prays that the Ephesian church comprehends this fullness, is strengthened by it and "filled up to all the fullness of Christ" (Eph. 3:19).

What God the Father brought to man is Jesus the great mediator. What man needs to bring to the Father is faith in this One who knows the way back. "No one comes to the Father but by Me" (John 14:6).

What's the Message?

Ex. 25–30

Man Needs What God Provides

When sin succeeded to mar the image God had made of Himself, God came looking for man, and He still is (John 6:44). Since carnal man sees no need for God, he does not look for Him. He prefers to hide behind the common grace God gives to all men. Common grace is like manna. Everyone gathered it and ate it and sometimes appreciated it.

But God also provided another type of food in the holy place. Those who ministered to Him there were privileged to eat of the "bread of the presence." This is a more abundant provision of nearness to God than common grace. It is a privilege enjoyed by them only after they understand their own need for what God provides.

The instructions God gave to Moses for the construction of the tabernacle revealed that they needed a divinely *appointed mediator* who would speak both truth and grace to them.

They needed *atonement* by an innocent victim, which provided a way of approach by the shedding of blood.

They needed *to know* the terms of covenant communion to walk humbly with their God.

They needed *a mercy seat* where God Himself would fulfill the law and guard its perfection.

They needed *to understand* that the holiness and glory of Jehovah was watched over by cherubim.

They needed *to be aware* of the revelation of God's character and his hatred for sin and His justice in judging sin, even while He justified sinners.

They needed *to comprehend* that God was light, and the tabernacle was a place of light.

They needed *to distinguish* between the light of the outer court, which was natural sunlight and the light in the holy place, which was provided by the lampstand—Jesus, the light of the world. And then there was the light of the holy of holies, which was the Shekinah glory of Jehovah.

The tabernacle then also revealed God's provision for all these needs.

> The way into righteousness is illustrated at the gate.
>
> The means of redemption is illustrated at the altar of sacrifice.
>
> The washing of sanctification is illustrated at the laver.
>
> The holy place for satisfaction is illustrated at the table of bread.
>
> The holy place for illumination is illustrated at the lampstand.
>
> The holy place for intercession is illustrated at the altar of incense.
>
> The most holy place for mercy and grace is illustrated at the ark of the covenant, the dwelling place of God and guardian of the law.

The order in which the tabernacle is presented to Moses begins at the mercy seat in the holy of holies and moves toward man outside the gate.

It is man who needed a way of approach to the mercy seat, so the journey for the sinner was from the gate in the outer court to the holy of holies; from the place of sin to perfection and from grace to glory.

The following list is not meant to describe everything in detail, but it is sufficient to illustrate that Jesus is more than just someone who died for us. God intended all this to be put on and enjoyed by the believer.

We go wrong when we tend to specialize or emphasize one or some of these ministries of Christ above others. By doing so, we become *living frauds*. The Jesus of the tabernacle is not a supermarket. We are not given the liberty to pick out what we like and ignore the rest.

He first presents what is brought to man in Jesus Christ

The type of Christ	The provisions of Christ for the believer
Ex. 25:10: The Ark	The Glory of Christ
Ex. 25:17: The Mercy seat over the law	The justice of Christ
Ex. 25:23: The Table of showbread	The delight of Christ
Ex. 25:25: The Lamp stand	The enlightenment of Christ
Ex. 26:1: The Curtains	The character of Christ
Ex. 26:15 The boards – gold	The deity of Christ
wood	The humanity of Christ
Ex: 26:19 The silver sockets	The atonement of Christ
Ex. 26:36 The veil	The warnings of Christ
Ex. 27:1 The bronze altar	The redemption of Christ
Ex. 27:9 The curtain of the courts	The righteousness of Christ
Ex. 27:16 The gate	The invitation of Christ
Ex. 27:17 The bronze sockets	The judgments of Christ

Then He provides for man the mediation of the priesthood to return with Him to the holy place.

Ex. 27:20 The pure olive oil	The Spirit of Christ
Ex. 28:1 The priests' garments	The position of Christ
Ex. 30:1 The altar of incense	The intercession of Christ
Ex. 30:17 The Laver for daily washing	The sanctification of Christ
Ex. 30:22 The anointing oil for ministry	The authority of Christ
Ex. 30:34 The incense for worship	The acceptance of Christ

The Lord Called

Book of Leviticus

Listen and Open Your Hands

Where Exodus concludes, Leviticus carries on with the words *Then the Lord called,"* which is the Hebrew title. Given over a period of one month (Ex. 40:17; Num. 1:1), the instructions were from the mercy seat, where the glory of God now rested. He spoke to Moses as an expression of the *need for a mediator.* With the exception of the events of chapters 9 and 10, the book is a direct quotation from God.

Already in the first part of this book, as it describes the offerings and sacrifices and priesthood, we see that:

> The holiness of God demanded a sacrifice.
> The majesty of God required regulations.
> The honor of God necessitated a code of conduct.
> The perfection of God expected the best of its kind.
> The purity of God deserved freedom from blemish.
> The sovereignty of God meant obedience to detail.

Nothing was left to man's imagination or interpretation.

In Exodus, in the tabernacle of grace we can see the truth of Israel's *position.* They were God's people, and He was providing the way to holiness in giving Israel what they did not deserve.

In Leviticus, in the offerings and sacrifices we the see the truth about Israel's *condition.* God was providing the mercy of identification and substitution; not giving Israel what they did deserve.

The book begins by describing the first of five different offerings.

In *the burnt offering*, we see the work of Jesus in consecrating Himself to God the Father's requirements for perfect holiness, as required in the first great commandment. He was consecrated to love the Lord His God with all His heart, soul, mind and strength.

In *the meal offering*, we see the work of Jesus consecrating Himself to fulfill the needs of man. He displayed the meaning of the second great commandment, which is to love His neighbor as Himself.

In *the sin offering*, we see Him in substitution, in the place of the sinner for the unintentional sin of ignorance toward God.

In *the trespass offering*, we see Him in restoration of the honor of the law that had been broken in man's relationship to man.

In *the peace offering*, we see reconciliation and peace with God.

In chapters nine and ten, we see *the inauguration of Aaron* and his four sons to the priesthood, and the instant death of two of them for using fire from a source other than the burnt offering. (Lev. 10:2).

In chapters 11–16, we see the love of God jealously compelling Israel to come to Him by:

Lev. 11: revealing the discernment of sin in clean and unclean animals.

Lev. 12: revealing the transmission of sin in childbirth.

Lev. 13: revealing the effects of sin in the disease of leprosy.

Lev. 14: revealing the restoration from sin in healing from leprosy.

Lev. 15: revealing the secret and original sin in the flowing discharge.

Lev. 16: revealing the atonement for sin at the sixth of seven annual feasts where all the sin of Israel was covered over.

I think God was filling Israel's hands with all that was intended for them to understand. They were to be holy with intensive force.

In the consecration of the priesthood, this was also illustrated. The priest was fully set apart for all the duties and privileges of his office.

The instructions of Ex. 29 were carried out in Lev 8. They too held their hands open to be filled with everything that belonged to God. Ex. 29:22–25. They were to minister this fullness to Israel.

The Hebrew term for this consecration is "filling the hand." In the book of Hebrews, this thought of the consecration of Jesus is expressed in the English "making perfect."

Notice the use of this phrase "making perfect" in the following references.

First Christ is spoken of as *being made perfect.* He was being consecrated. He had His hands filled as did the priests of old. This is what is referred to in Heb. 2:10 where we read " . . . to perfect the author of their salvation through suffering." This refers to His obedience to His Father during His three year ministry, not His sinless character.

Then we read in Heb. 5:9–10 *"and having been made perfect."* Here He is designated by God as high priest. This is at the conclusion of His ministry.

Next we read in Heb. 7:28, " . . . *appoints a Son made perfect forever."* This is at His ascension.

In Heb. 10:14; " . . . *Has perfected for all time* those who are sanctified." Jesus puts them into possession of all the privileges of the fully pardoned and justified ones. This is applied to all believers.

And lastly in Heb. 12:23, " . . . *and to the spirits of righteous men made perfect."* They fully enter into the possession of all that was intended for them. This is in the coming everlasting kingdom.

In James 2:22 we read of Abraham that " ... as a result of his works *faith was perfected,*" meaning that his faith was carried out to its full intent.

I John 2:5 says," Whoever keeps His word, in Him *the love of God has truly been perfected.*" It is carried out to its intended purpose.

God was filling Jesus' hands with everything that was intended for Him and applies its benefits to all believers. In this way, God's love to us has reached its perfection. John expands on this blessing in I John 4:17, saying " ... as He is so also are we."

When *the Lord calls,* do we open our hands in front of us? Are we willing for God to fill them with the duties and privileges He intended?

It is possible to open them only for His blessing, not His fullness.

Assigning Responsibility
Book of Numbers
"In The Wilderness"

In Leviticus, the three-fold law has been greatly expanded upon, emphasizing mainly the ceremonial laws that governed religious life. The book of "Numbers" in Greek, or "In the Wilderness" in Hebrew, expands on the civil laws that governed national life.

In Leviticus, Moses is 30 days receiving instructions on the offerings, sacrifices, and feasts from the mercy seat of the ark.

In Numbers, he is 39 years in leading, judging and teaching.

The book begins with God setting the affairs of Israel in order by taking a census of every male over 20 years old who is able to fight in war.

He places the numbers of Israel by tribe in camps around the presence of God in the tabernacle in the form of a cross. This was well over a thousand years before the Romans began to use it as a means of punishment. The longest portion pointed east. The shortest portion pointed west. And the equal portions of the cross bar north and south. This encampment was an enormous tent city.

To the east are three tribes camped under the banner *Lion* of the tribe of Judah. The census counted 186,400 in the tribes of Issachar, Judah, Zebulon, plus Moses, Aaron and his two sons.

To the west are three tribes under the banner *Ox* of the tribe of Ephraim. The census counted 115,600 in the tribes of Manasseh, Ephraim and Benjamin, including 7500 Gershonite Levites.

To the south are three tribes under the banner *Man* of the tribe Reuben. The census counted 160,050 in the tribes of Simeon, Reuben, and Gad. including 8600 Kohathite Levites.

To the North are three tribes under the banner *Eagle* of the tribe Dan. The census counted 163,800 in the tribes of Asher, Dan, and Naphtali. including 6200 Merarite Levites.

In chapter 1:4–10 Ezekiel looks north and sees four living beings with human form. In their faces, each had the face of a man (south) the face of a lion on the right (east), the face of a bull or ox on the left (west), and the face of an eagle (north).

In Revelation 4:7, we see the same description around the throne in heaven. Day and night they say, "holy, holy, holy is the Lord God the Almighty who was and is to come."

In contrast, we read of curiosity, murmuring, grumbling, complaining and arguing around the tabernacle at mount Horeb. Into this gulf between heaven and earth came a mediator.

Matthew presents Him as *King of the Jews.* It was written for Jews expecting their Messiah King. The kingdom of heaven is mentioned 54 times. He is spoken of as "the Lion that is from the tribe of Judah, the root of David" in Rev. 5:5. It corresponds to the *face of the lion,* which is often thought of as king of the animals.

Mark presents Him as *the Servant.* He emphasizes the ministry of Jesus as a servant, what Jesus did instead of what He said and uses servant language like "immediately" Of the 41 times "immediately" is used in the four gospels, Mark uses it 17 times. It corresponds to the *face of the ox,* an animal thought of and used for lowly service and hard work.

Luke presents Him as *Son of Man.* He emphasizes the humanity of Jesus in His birth and childhood, His great interest in people like Zaccheus, the prodigal son, the publican, Samaritans, lepers, the ministry of women and the need of prayer. It corresponds to *the face of a man.*

John presents Him as *Son of God.* He emphasizes the deity of Jesus in phrases like, "the Word was God," "the Lamb of God," "the Messiah," and the "I am" claims like, "I am the bread that came down from heaven." It corresponds to *the face of an eagle.*

If God's will was to be done on earth as it was in heaven, then God would be very intentional about how and by whom He was surrounded, even though it may have been a mystery to man.

In Numbers 3, 4 and 8, God takes the Levites, instead of the firstborn of Israel, and assigns them the responsibilities in all the service of the tabernacle. The *Gershonite* and *Merarite* Levites transported some 20 tons of material on six wagons. The *Kohathites* carried the furniture.

Chapter 10 gives the tribal order while traveling between camps. Divine guidance does not exclude order or human responsibility.

Chapter 12 presents Gods' view of Moses, the appointed mediator as a type of Christ, the most humble man on the face of the earth. God speaks of Moses as a friend (Ex. 33:11; Num. 12:6–8) as He did of Abraham (Jam. 2:23). Yet Moses was refused entry into the land of promise for the *one failure of striking the Rock twice* with the rod instead of speaking to it (Num 20:8). In Ex. 17:6, he was to strike the rock. Jesus the Rock was beaten once for living water to flow. We now are just to speak to Him.

The next seventeen chapters record Israel's desert wanderings during the forty years they were led by the cloud and pillar of fire.

Chapters 28 and 29 remind Israel of the seven annual feasts, also recorded in Lev. 23. These foreshadowed the entire history of God's redemption plan. We await the fulfillment of these last three feasts.

God gave all the necessary instructions for His people, knowing they would need them in the years to come. Some of God's dealings with us are also laying necessary foundations as preparation for future events and circumstances we are presently unaware of.

In chapter 34, God sets the boundaries for the land and the allotted cities for the Levites and refugees who need a place to flee.

There will be times in our lives when *we also will see our own failures* in assigned responsibilities or grumbling unbelief and in need of a place of refuge. These failures will find us in our wilderness wanderings or when we are settled in God's provisions.

Progression of Sin
Rom. 6:14
"No More Has Dominion Over You"

The book of Leviticus is a very graphic picture of what God thinks of sin and how He intends to deal with it. Those who are unfamiliar with God's view tend to think of sin quite often as a very gratifying experience, at least for while—usually until God comes for a visit or they see the consequences of the *lust of the flesh* (Ex.16:3), *lust of the eyes* (Gen. 13:10), *pride of life* (Dan. 4:30). We are all conceived and born subject to these. But in God's presence, they cease to be pleasant.

There is another ugly aspect of sin. Not only is it always active, it is *progressive*. Ps. 19:12–13 illustrates this for us.

David begins this Psalm by saying the heavens declare the glory of God and continues for six verses. It is called *general revelation*. It doesn't talk, write, or argue, but the apostle Paul says that, "we can know God through the things He has made" (Rom. 1:19). Next he writes about the law of the Lord for five verses. This is God's *special revelation*. It relates very specific things about God. All scripture does this (II Tim. 3:16).

The third kind is the *revelation the Spirit of God brings* and is presented to us in verses 12–13. This brings the deepest awareness of sin, its effect and progressive control over us. Five stages of sin are mentioned.

Errors are not intentional. *Hidden faults* are known sins, but kept secret. *Presumptuous sins* are known and practiced, but are presumed to be without consequence. Then there are sins that rule over us. We are addicted. We can't stop. They have *dominion over us.* We are slaves to it. And lastly there is *the sin of great transgression.* We blame God or Satan or neighbor as if it is their fault. Each of these kinds of sin successively brings its greater power of control over us.

So who can discern his errors and all the results that flow from it? The Spirit of God can. He takes the Word of God, "which is living and active . . . and is able to judge the thoughts and intentions of the heart" (Heb. 4:12) and applies it for teaching, correction, comfort, etc.

Almost 700 years before the letter to the Hebrews was written, Jeremiah the prophet declared a similar message in 17:9–10.

> "The heart is more deceitful than all else and desperately sick; Who can understand it? I the Lord search the heart, I test the mind, Even to give to each man according to his ways . . ."

God is not just looking to prove that we sin. He wants to keep us from going deeper into sin and lead us into His presence instead.

For this, there is a rebirth that provides us with deliverance from:

> The pollution of sin—a fountain for sin and impurity (Zech. 13:1).

> The penalty of sin—blood was put on the doorposts, and the angel of death passed over them (Ex. 12:13).

> The power of sin—the power of Egypt's army destroyed (Ex. 14:30–31).

The power of death–the Jordan river in flood stage was crossed by Israel (Josh. 3:16). The flood of judgment against Adams' sin (death) is stopped by God's presence on the ark as the priests' feet touch the water.

As we now approach the *tabernacle court,* we will see what God the Father provided for us in Jesus to affect this change. Paul writes of this in I Cor. 2:2: "I determined to know nothing among you except Jesus Christ and Him crucified." He emphasizes two things: Everything the Father brought to man in Jesus Christ, and everything Jesus provides for man as He brings and restores us into fellowship with God.

To follow Him there will require the heeding of His warning, "And he who does not *take his cross* and *follow after Me* is not worthy of Me" (Matt. 10:38; 16:24).

Why is this cross so important for following after Jesus? Why does it have so many enemies that are offended by it and despise and reject it? (Phil. 3:18). I'll let Paul answer the question.

I Cor. 1:18–*"For the word of the cross is to those who are perishing foolishness, but to us who are being saved it is the power of God."* The cross is powerful, for it satisfied the needs of God and man.

Gal. 5:11–*"If I preach circumcision why am I persecuted? Then the stumbling block of the cross has been abolished."* The cross offends.

Gal. 6:12–*"They try to compel you to be circumcised, simply that they may not be persecuted for the cross of Christ."* It brings persecution.

Gal. 6:14–*"That I should never boast except in the cross of our Lord Jesus Christ through which the world has been crucified in me and I to the world."* The cross kills every carnal thing.

Eph. 2:16–*"and might reconcile them both in one body to God through the cross, by it having put to death the enmity between races."* The cross reconciles the conflicts between enemies.

Phil. 2:8–*"He humbled Himself by becoming obedient to the point of death, even death on a cross."* The cross humbles us to submission.

Col. 1:20–*"to reconcile all things to Himself, having made peace through the blood on the cross."* The cross reestablishes the peace between God and man that was lost.

Col. 2:14–*"having cancelled out the certificate of debt - he has taken it out of the way having nailed it to the cross."* The cross testifies that the debt man owed to God is paid in full.

Heb. 12:2–*"fixing our eyes on Jesus . . . who endured the cross,"* This teaches us to take up our cross, " . . . because he who has suffered in the flesh has ceased from sin" (I Peter 4:1). The cross bears witness of its lasting effect.

In the cross *the dominion of sin is broken* in practical experience.

The Boundaries
Exodus 19:12
Until Christ Is Formed In You
Gal. 4:19

There was a remarkable difference between Moses and Israel. Moses was the humblest man on earth. (Num. 12:3). In his prayer of Ex. 33:13, he asks, *"let me know your ways that I may know You"* and verse 18, "show me your glory," to which God agrees. Whenever God called, Moses would go into the "tent of the presence or meeting," which was outside the camp, (perhaps near the clean place) to speak with God.

Israel was of a different heart. After their first encounter with God's voice (Ex. 20:19), the people said to Moses, "speak to us yourself and we will listen; *but let not God speak to us* lest we die." Here were a few million people who were willing to follow the instructions of Moses, their mediator, but they were too fearful to hear from God themselves.

The consequence was significant. God, knowing the heart of His people, instructed Moses to *"set boundaries for the people* all around saying, 'Beware that you do not go up on the mountain or touch the border of it. Whoever touches the mountain shall be put to death." (Ex. 19:12). So Moses instructed the people to prepare for God to come down onto the mountain on the third day. Up until this present occasion, He had silently enacted His miracles. Now He was to speak to them audibly from the mountain.

In verse 20, Moses was called up again, then sent down to again warn about the boundary and to return with Aaron (verse

24). While he was down this time, God spoke the Ten Commandments, and the millions of Israel heard it.

What was so important about this boundary? Why the trips up and down the mountain? *Why could Moses cross the boundary while God was so adamant that Israel was not to even touch this boundary on penalty of death?* Were they not all His people, descendants of Abraham? Was this the only time and place in history where God set a boundary for His people so they had to remain a distance from Him?

Was it the humility of Moses that gave him access (Num. 12:3)? Why could only the high priest go into the holy of holies once a year? Why were priests allowed no nearer than the veil? The Israelites no further than the altar? Why were only the Kohathites to carry the furniture of the tabernacle? Why were the ladies allowed no nearer than the gate of the outer court (Ex. 38:8)? Was Hanna not far more humble and holy than Eli the high priest and his two sons (I Sam. 2:27–36)? Why all these boundaries?

Besides God's electing purposes, Moses had undergone a remarkable change from his first attempt to free his people until 40 years later when he was still herding sheep for his father in law.

Moses had become quite a friend of God (Num. 12). The next forty years in a wilderness would make Israel quite a different nation, also. Jesus himself went into the wilderness *full of the Holy Spirit.* (Luke 4:1). He came out 40 days later, *full of the power of the Holy Spirit* (Luke 4:14).

Learning to walk with God requires wilderness experience. As long as we have a contemporary mind, (the mind of our culture, like Egypt in the mind of Israel), we will not mature past being interested in God to help us with our sin-created problems. A comfortable pew is no substitute for 40 years of

Enabled by Pardon

separation and of being set apart for the purpose and intent of God for our life. Moses was 40 years ahead of Israel in having the mind and humility of Christ. The consecrated mind of faith in God's promises is rooted in love and trust, the abandonment of self into God's care.

Some common boundaries we all face everyday are:

Mouth—the anger of man does not achieve the
        righteousness of God" (James 3:8–12).
        We need to get the tongue under control.

Love—"If I Have not love, it profits me nothing"
        (I Cor. 13).
Extreme obedience without extravagant love profits nothing.

Faith—"Without faith it is impossible to please God"
        (Heb. 11:6). God is jealous for His glory,
        so faith must be carried out to its
        intended purpose.
Mind— "Be transformed by the renewing of your mind"
        (Rom. 12:2).
We need to learn the thoughts of God from the word of God.

Heart— "The heart is deceitful above all things and
        desperately wicked; who can know it"
                (Jer. 17:9 NKJV). "The sacrifices of
                God are a broken spirit, A broken and
                a contrite heart- These, O God, you
                will not despise" (Ps 51:17 NKJV).
God knows our hearts far better than we do.

Music—"And they ministered with song before the
        tabernacle of the tent of meeting, until Solomon
        had built the house of the Lord . . ."

53

> *(I Chron. 6:32). " . . . and all the Levitical*
> *singers . . . with cymbals, harps, and lyres,*
> *standing east of the altar"*–(II Chron 5:12).

God gave the musicians a location from which to sing before Him. The latest good ideas were not allowed to be brought into the holy place. Not by the priests or musicians.

The only things allowed into the holy place were the consecrations of the priests; oil for the lamp stand; bread, wine, and incense for the table; incense for the altar; and blood. Everything that was brought into the holy place was a type of Christ. Nothing else was acceptable to God.

Our cultural thinking assumes that we are basically good people who just need to fix up a few things. God make no such compromises with His own holy perfections.

Therefore it is important to: "gather together in My name" (Matt. 18:23), "do a miracle in My name" (Mark 9:39), "give a cup of water in My name" (Mark 9:41), "receive this child in My name" (Luke 9:48), "ask in My name" (John 14:13). It is *His name and the life it represents* that is the only way to the Father without boundaries.

The Two Masters

Matt. 6:24

I must be as desperate to have God accept me as a
sinner as I am desperate to accept God's holiness.

The above quote distinguishes two distinct aspects of having *one Master*. God's acceptance of me as a sinner and my acceptance of God's holiness both need to be my master.

Jesus mentions this distinction in Matt. 23:21.

> "And He who swears by the temple, swears both by the temple and by Him who dwells within it."

The temple was considered to be *holy and sacred*, while God who lived in it was *merciful and gracious* and accepting of sinners on the merits of Christ's life. The pride of carnal flesh is quite opposed to this.

In the story of Balaam (Num. 22–25), we can see this opposition. There are not two aspects of one master but *two masters* in one man. And flesh wants to exert its influence over Spirit.

Peter mentions *the way of Balaam.* (II Peter 2:15). He was willing to compromise God's higher morality by getting the Midianites to invite Israel to their worship feasts. Though he spoke what God told him to say while prophesying (spirit), he did mention something on the side that God had not inspired him to say (flesh) (Num. 31:16).

He knew that what God would not let him pronounce as a curse, he would accomplish by getting God to judge the adultery of Israel, and 24,000 people in Israel died. Balaam also paid his own penalty for this (Num. 31:8).

In Jude 1:11, there is the warning of *the error of Balaam.* He used his gift of prophecy to gain material wealth–he commercialized his gift. As Jude says" . . . for pay they have rushed headlong into the error of Balaam." The gift of God made him important and influential, but with it came the temptation to compromise on God's holiness. He chose not to resist.

The church in Pergamum held to *the doctrine, or "teaching of Balaam"* (Rev. 2:14), eating things sacrificed to idols and committing acts of immorality.

Balaam's teaching was already in the early church–be user friendly; make a few compromises; nobody's perfect; don't be a "holier than you" separatist; don't listen to Peter's comment, "You are a chosen race, a royal priesthood, a holy nation, a people for God's own possession" (I Pet. 2:9).

Balaam's teaching says, "You can worship flesh and Spirit." The wisdom of man's flesh has always gravitated toward despising and rejecting the foolishness of the cross and Spirit of Christ.

For the Romans in 12:2, Paul points to the effect of the two masters of flesh and Spirit *on their thinking.*

> "And do not be conformed to this world, but be transformed by the renewing of your mind."

He warns the Galatians in 5:16–17 of the effect *on their conduct.*

> "But I say, walk by the Spirit, and you will not carry out the desires of the flesh. For the flesh sets its desires against the Spirit, and the Spirit against the flesh; for these are in opposition to one another, so you may not do the things that you please."

He then gives a list of consequences in verses 19–21.

Think of the effect it has had *on our culture* to teach evolution instead of creation. David, who was inspired to write many of the Psalms, writes in Ps. 139:16 (NKJV):

> "Your eyes saw my substance being yet unformed. And in Your book they all were written, The days fashioned for me, when as yet there was none of them."

What a contrast to the theory of *flesh having evolved* by a series of beneficial accidents.

Think of the different priorities held by people who pursue the *gift* of God and those who pursue the *inheritance* of God. Peter in I Pet. 1:4 talks about "obtaining an *inheritance* which is imperishable and undefiled and will not fade away, reserved in heaven for you." In contrast, Paul speaks of *gifts* that will be done away with (I Cor.13:8). God's holiness needs to be master of both.

The life stories of two kings will illustrate what a difference it makes to pursue God's good gift apart from the inheritance.

King Saul was given kingship as *a gift* (I Sam.10). With this gift he established a national army and defeated enemies in battle. But his gift of kingship was more important than obedience, holiness or his inheritance.

David was also anointed king during Saul's reign, but he had the anointing as *an inheritance* until Saul's death. While Saul pursued and hunted for him, David never tried to take kingship from Saul, even when Saul lay asleep at his feet for a second time (I Sam. 24:6; 26:7). David simply says, "The Lord forbid that I should stretch out my hand against the Lord's anointed" (verse 11).

While Saul did everything he could to use and keep his gift

of kingship, David trusted in God to fulfill His promised inheritance. He pursued his relationship with God, even though he was already anointed as king. While God's *gift of kingship* could not change the heart of Saul–*it could only reveal what was in it*–David's inheritance of God's plan for him was safe and secure from Saul's attacks and established him in a unique relationship of trust and favor with God.

Paul makes a similar distinction in I Cor. 14:1. Pursue love, yet desire earnestly spiritual gifts. The love is described in chapter 13, the gifts in chapter 12. *The pursuing of love* covers a multitude of sin (I Pet. 4:8). The *absence of it* means I contribute nothing (I Cor. 13:1), I am nothing (verse 2), it profits me nothing (verse 3).

We each need to know our gift and use it to minister to others. But gifts can also be badly abused since "the gift and the calling of God are irrevocable" (Rom. 11:29). So *pursue the love of God* that provides His *gift* of grace to accept sinners. And make *the inheritance of God's holiness* the means by which the gift of God is ministered to others.

"The Court"

Ex. 27:9

Bring In Everlasting Righteousness Dan. 9:24

In the midst of all the black spun goat hair tents of Israel's encampment was a white linen curtain around the perimeter of a court of 100 by 50 cubits (about 50 by 25 meters). This curtain was upheld and put on display by wooden poles.

In Song of Solomon 3:6–11, the traveling couch of Solomon is coming up from the wilderness with 60 of the mighty men of Israel around it. Its interior was decorated by the women of Jerusalem.

There is a remarkable similarity of this to the tabernacle of God in the wilderness. This was His resting place surrounded by 60 wooden poles. He, too, was bringing His bride into her new dwelling place. But this was a place of everlasting righteousness made without human hands.

Inside this court was the *"tent of meeting"* (Ex. 40:6), the appointed meeting place for His people. In front of it were the altar and the laver. These foreshadowed Jesus as being accessible on earth to all who sought Him. "Blessed is the man You choose, and cause to approach You" (Ps. 65:4 NJKV). Both the Jews and Gentiles had the same access. " . . . as you are, so shall the alien be before the Lord" (Num. 15:15).

The poles were 60 in number, which is 5 times 12. *Five is the number for grace*, and *twelve is perfect government*. It is the grace of God reigning in perfect righteousness by Jesus Christ.

They were *made of wood,* which speaks of the humanity of Jesus.

These *stood in bronze* sockets. The bronze testifies of endurance. It has the capacity to bear the action of fire, which typifies Jesus, not consumed by God's judgment against sin.

Silver caps covered the tops of the poles, and silver hooks were attached to them. Silver rails (connecting rods) extended horizontally from pole to pole. Silver is the symbol of atonement and means "to cover." From these rails was suspended the white linen curtain.

Every five cubits stood a pole five cubits high. Here for all to see was Jesus *(wooden poles)* standing in the place of judgment *(bronze sockets)*, covered with the atonement of a ransom paid *(silver caps),* and displaying the union of grace *(five)* and righteousness. *(white linen)*

The *white linen* of the court was the same length as the inner curtains which spread over the tabernacle. The court was 280 cubits around its perimeter, while there were 10 ribbons of 28 cubits over the tabernacle.

Inside the holy place the righteousness of Jesus was presented to the eye of the Father. It covered and surrounded His dwelling place and *rested on* the atoning work of Christ (silver sockets under the boards).

Outside, the righteousness of Jesus was presented to the eye of man. There the white linen was suspended from the silver rails around the court and pointed the way to the gate.

It is the unrighteous human race that is in need of being clothed in righteousness. They need to *look up* to see that this righteousness (white linen) is always upheld by the great work of atonement (silver caps and rails).

The white linen for the court was a boundary between holy and carnal. It was a barrier to those outside and protection for those inside.

A sinner comes to Christ so that, "grace might reign through righteousness to eternal life through Jesus Christ our Lord" (Rom. 5:21).

Isaiah testifies of this in chapter 61:10:

> "I will rejoice greatly in the Lord, My soul will exult in My God; For He has clothed me with garments of salvation, He has wrapped me with a robe of righteousness."

John, in his vision of things to come, writes in Rev. 19:8:

> "And it was given to her to clothe herself in fine linen, bright and clean, for the fine linen is the righteous acts of the saints."

Righteousness is a purity of heart, a holiness, a perfect obedience to the law. The life of Jesus Christ demonstrated this.

Holiness is a separation from evil; *righteousness addresses* this evil.

"And Abraham believed God and it was imputed unto him for righteousness" (Rom. 4:3). Jesus' righteousness was reckoned to him.

Unbelief is to wear the robe of our self-righteous pride. It looks like a filthy rag compared to His pure, fine, white, bright, clean linen (Is. 64:6).

In I Sam. 18:4, Jonathan and David enter into a covenant. There is an exchange of a few items. One of these is the robe Jonathan takes off as prince of Israel, heir to the throne of his father King Saul, and he puts it on David.

As part of this covenant ceremony, David, now wearing this robe, *became by a legal enactment heir to the throne of Israel.*

When we are drawn by the Father to enter by faith through

the gate, we find ourselves in the court where the righteousness of Christ is imputed to us. His robe of righteousness is placed on us, making us heirs of the kingdom of God, while He took upon Himself our robes (rags) of sin.

He invites and draws us in.

> "Behold I stand at the door and knock; if anyone hears My voice and opens the door, I will come in to him, and will dine with him, and he with Me."–Rev. 3:20

Included in this transaction is the wonder of rebirth by the Spirit of God (John 3:16), and the promise of eternal privileges and responsibilities.

> "Truly I say to you who have followed Me, in the regeneration when the Son of Man will sit on His glorious throne, you also shall sit upon twelve thrones, judging the twelve tribes of Israel."–Matt. 19:28

Enter Through the Gate
Ex 27:16

The Master Has Come And He Calls For You
John 11:28

Jesus, the Master who calls for you, has good credentials.

He could feed the multitudes with bread and fish (John 6:9), teach the beatitudes (Matt. 5), and illustrate His Father's kingdom (Matt. 20:1). He demonstrated Himself master over sickness and disease (Matt. 4:23), wind and wave (Luke 8:24). He had authority to forgive sin (Mark 2:10), cast out demons (Luke 8:33), change water into wine (John 2:10), and raise the dead. (John 11:43). He could clean up a person's past addictions to sin, transform the ordinary, every day life experience of getting water from a well into drinking living water from heaven's well, and make what was temporary the eternal.

This is the Master who calls us. And it is beneficial to welcome His purpose and will for us:

> *The I will of cleansing.* "I am willing, be cleansed" (Luke 5:13 NKJV). Leprosy was such a vivid picture of the evidence of sin.

> *The I will of possession.* "Is it not lawful for me to do what I wish with what is my own" (Matt. 20:15). Is the world and everything in it not His? Is He not entitled to own you?

> *The I will of subordination.* "If I will that he remain 'til I come, what is that to you? You follow me" (John 21:22 NKJV). Should He not be allowed to tell us where to go and what to do with our life?

The I will of glorification. "I will that they also . . . be with Me where I am" (John 17:24 KJV). His prayer is that I should spend eternity with Him.

The response of Mary to the Master's call was that she arose quickly to meet the Master. He waits at the gate.

He has put all this white linen on display all around for all to see His righteousness and grace. It is meant to lead us to the gate.

It is a *wide gate*, 20 cubits or about 10 meters. Wide enough for "Whoever will call upon the name of the Lord . . ." (Rom. 10:13). to use as entrance into the court.

Though it was hanging down from the silver rails, it was never locked. An act of faith could open it. Hebrews 11:6 says it is impossible to please God without it. Just pull the curtain aside of this *only gate*, since " . . . no one comes to the Father but by Me" (John 14:6).

No one enters in on personal credentials. It is for the humble who know they need help. " . . . whoever humbles himself shall be exalted" (Matt. 23:12). Those who will enter this gate, will also see a second entrance leading into the holy place. It is only half as wide but twice as high, and there are not many who care to enter it.

The first entrance was low but colorful and attractive. There were four colors: *white linen* with a *blue, purple and scarlet (red)* pattern woven into it (Ex. 26:31). These colors are emphasized first here as well as in the veil (Ex. 27:16). They speak of the Redeemer and His glorious attributes. For the inner curtain that covered the holy place, the *white linen* is mentioned first (Ex. 26:1). The white linen in each place where it is used emphasizes His character of perfect righteousness.

Purple speaks of His Kingship. Matthew emphasizes the King and His kingdom, the Kinsman Redeemer. Fifty-four times Matthew uses the term "Kingdom of Heaven," and many of the parables are about the kingdom. He records the geneology of the Son of David. The magi asked, "Where is He that is born King of the Jews?" Over His cross was written, "King of the Jews." He presents Jesus as Lord and King. *This ought to be our testimony.*

Scarlet speaks of His servanthood. Mark emphasizes Jesus as a servant. He uses servant language like "immediately" 17 times. Scarlet is the color of blood. The dye comes from a worm called a scarlet worm, and David uses this image as he prophesies of Jesus in Ps. 22:6: "But I am a worm and no man." Mark emphasizes what Jesus did instead of what He said. *This ought to be our ministry.*

White linen speaks of His righteous humanity. Luke emphasizes the humanity of Jesus. He records the events around His birth, the relatives, the shepherds, the flight to Egypt and His boyhood time in the temple. He records the Songs of Elizabeth, Mary, Simeon and the ministry of John the Baptist. He represents Jesus as the compassionate Son of Man. *This ought to be our character.*

Blue speaks of His divinity. John emphasizes Jesus as the Son of God who came down from heaven and satisfied the demands of God for holy perfection. He calls Him Lamb of God, the Messiah, King of Israel, Savior of the world, Lord and God. He presents Jesus in a series of "I am's" (John 6:35, 8:12, 9:5). *This ought to be our Vision of Christ.*

The gate speaks to us of repentance, which is inseparable from faith. Without some measure of faith, no one has the capacity or the desire to repent. Entry through this gate enables one to understand how great the grace of God was that drew us in (John 6:44).

Repentance is a turning toward God on account of sin. A grieving over what were once the pleasures of sin. A humble self-surrender to the intended purpose of God for our life. It is a definite turning from going our own way, seeking our own pleasure and speaking our own words. This was seen in the life and testimony of Jesus (John 5:19,30). God accepts no other way.

"I am the door of the sheep" (John 10:7). "Come, you who are blessed of my Father, inherit the kingdom prepared for you from the foundation of the world" (Matt. 25:34). God provided no other entrance way into His presence.

For We Who Have Believed

Heb. 4:3

Enter Into That Rest of His Righteousness

One needs to have a high view of God to believe and trust Him. Wishful thinking and opinions do not qualify us for entry through the gate. They cannot give us rest. But God's gifts and promises do.

While *the gifts of God* become operational by an act of the will, *the promises of God* become operational by an act of trusting faith. Both the will and faith are necessary for a functional Christian life. Paul, in writing his first letter to the Thessalonians (5:13–18 NKJV), outlines various duties and behaviors in which both need to be operational.

> "Be at peace among yourselves . . . warn those who are unruly, comfort the faint hearted, uphold the weak, be patient with all. See that no one renders evil for evil to anyone, but always pursue what is good . . . Rejoice always, pray without ceasing, in everything give thanks; . . . Do not quench the Spirit. Do not despise prophecies. Test all things; hold fast what is good. Abstain from every form of evil."

When either the will or faith or both of them are absent, the list looks very different–immorality, impurity, sensuality, idolatry, sorcery, enmities, strife, jealousy, outbursts of anger, etc. to mention a few from Gal. 5:19–21.

Isaiah recognizes the need *to will* and *to trust* in order to enter the place of rest. In Isa. 30:15 he provides us with a summary.

"In repentance and rest you shall be saved. In quietness and trust is your strength. But you were not willing."

Repentance is an act of the will enabled by grace to trust.

For the millions who left Egypt, there was a failure to enact the gift of God by an act of the will or the promises of God by an act of faith, or both.

Only two of all those over twenty years old crossed over the Jordan River into the provisions of God's promises. "The word they heard did not profit them because it was not united by faith in those who heard" (Heb. 4:2).

The hearts of the human race are like the four kinds of soil Jesus spoke of in Matt. 13:4–8. There is the hardened soil of a well-traveled roadway that becomes a rut with no vegetation. There is rocky soil without depth for its roots to find water and food for growth. There is a soil infested with the competition of weeds and thorns necessitating a fight for basic survival. And then there is the good soil of sufficient resources yielding a good crop. God's Word in the human heart is like a seed that depends on the treatment it receives from the soil's condition and competition from the weeds.

God values His Word. "He has remembered His covenant forever, the word which He commanded to a thousand generations" (Ps. 105:8). Rest in it!

Having entered through the gate, *it is His word that will have to be trusted and acted upon.* It has proven to be trustworthy.

The heart that yields itself to be searched by God's Word and Spirit, it's thoughts and intentions discerned and judged, will not always err and live in unbelief, but will be quickened and changed.

The warning of Heb. 3:10–"they do always err in their heart"–does not need to be my daily experience.

Think of the prophetic past that Jesus fulfilled in His life, as evidence that He foreknows the future and foretells it with perfect accuracy. Think of the promises He has made to us who believe in John 14:2–3,6 (NKJV).

> "In my Father's house are many mansions; . . . I go to prepare a place for you"

> "I will come again and receive you to myself; that where I am you may be also."

> "I am the way, the truth and the life."

What a contrast to the theory that we have evolved by a series of beneficial accidents!

In Luke 22:24 begins an *encouraging event* for all believers who enter through the gate into His promises by faith and willfully minister the gifts.

Jesus states that one of them would betray Him, which sets off a debate among them about who is the greatest. He contributes to the discussion by directing their thoughts to a much bigger issue threatening their freedom.

He said to Peter, "Simon, Simon, behold Satan has *demanded permission* to sift you like wheat, (*asked repeatedly* that all of you be given over to him out of the power and keeping of God), but *I have prayed for you*, (the verb tense *implies once*) that your faith may not fail you" (verse 32).

Peter insists he is ready for prison and death, to which Jesus responds that Peter would deny knowing Him three times.

That same night Peter did deny Jesus three times, and he weeps bitterly over his failure to keep the accepted and understood responsibilities implied by drinking from the cup of the new covenant Jesus had offered them. But Jesus had prayed that Peter's faith should not fail him.

Carnal Peter failed. His flesh, like the flesh of all the rest of humanity, will fail. But the faith of Peter was preserved for an everlasting testimony.

Just read Peter's opening statements in his first letter.

"According to the foreknowledge of God the Father," (verse 2). "He has caused us to be born again to a living hope" (verse 3). That's *our past election*.

"To obtain an inheritance imperishable and undefiled, which will not fade away reserved in heaven." (verse 4). *That's our future glorification.*

"Who are protected by the power of God through faith" (verse 5).

That's our present sanctification.

The prayer of Jesus, our intercessor, was answered. Peter was not given up out of the keeping power of God. His life became an enactment of both the *gifts* and *promises* of God. By faith enter through the gate into this rest.

Religion

Math. 15:3–20

"Any well traveled trail becomes a rut with no vegetation."

I don't remember where I read or heard this, but I have been on many trails around the world and know it is true.

When a person stands at the door of the tabernacle, it's decision time. *Outside* the gate, there are a multitude of well-traveled trails with no vegetation, with no life, and no fruit. Multitudes are going the same way, doing the same thing.

Inside, Jesus says, " . . . I came that they might have life, and have it abundantly" (John 10:10). Every step is on new vegetation releasing its pleasing aroma. There is no rut to follow. Not many walk here. He who directs our steps says, "If any man is thirsty let him come to Me and drink. He who believes in Me, as the Scripture said, from his innermost being shall flow rivers of living water." (John 7:37,38).

Jesus offered this to a huge crowd of people during the final day of the feast of tabernacles. Thousands of pilgrims came from all over to celebrate the feast of tabernacles, which marked the coming of the Messiah's rule from the temple as King of Kings and Lord of Lords.

The very Jesus the celebration pointed to stood in their midst and offered them the promised Spirit that was to come. Half a year later, thousands did become a river of life, but multitudes remained on their well-traveled trail. They failed to realize that:

"*Beliefs* determine *values,* which determine *judgments,* which determine *choices,* which determine *decisions,* which determine *character,* which determines *greatness or failure.*"

71

A story is recorded in Matt.19, and Luke18 of a rich young ruler who came to Jesus with a question left unanswered by Deut. 28:1–14. It stated that if you obey the commandments, you would be blessed.

Well, he was young and already rich and a ruler, but it had not answered his question about how to obtain eternal life. He must have observed in Jesus' life and manner and teaching that Jesus also was a keeper of the law, for he calls Jesus, "good teacher."

This rich man had a set of *beliefs* which led him to think that his position and accomplishments were because of his human virtues. "All these things I have kept" (Luke 18:20) he said.

We tend to gravitate in our thinking toward believing it was human cause and effect, not divine mercy and grace. The effort to keep all the commandments should have led him to this mercy and grace.

His *beliefs* determined that he *valued* his prosperity and power to rule and receiving honor from others. But what he valued did not answer his question—"what else must I do?"

It determined that he had to make a *judgment* that Jesus would have an answer to his unanswered question.

Most don't go to Him.

They follow the *majority* who say, "Everybody's doing it."

They look at *results* and say, "I am not hurting anybody."

They think only of *themselves* and say, "It's my life."

They live by peer *values* and say, "Times are changing."

They measure *frequency* and say, "Just this once it's okay."

They check their *conscience* and say, "I feel okay about it."

Some even go to *the scriptures* to "see what God says."

His beliefs had provided good insulation for himself, but no consolation for others. We all like to wrap our religious blankets around ourselves for comfort and leave the lost out in the cold of ignorance, but Jesus gave him a choice. Keep what you have or "sell your possessions . . . and come follow me."

It was *decision* time, and he decided there must be something wrong with Jesus' theology. He went away sadly. He may have become the great apostle Paul. We don't know. It is not recorded what he did later on with the answer. But there was not yet a place in his life for dependant faith.

This decision determined *character*. The god of such people is only as strong as their own strength, as wise as their own minds, and as good as the blessings which come to them.

For Jesus, faith, forgiveness of sin, and the evil one were things that revealed His character and drove Him to His Father in prayer each day.

While people primarily sought solutions to their problems, their poverty, illness and political oppression, Jesus focused on such human problems as pride, hypocrisy and legalism. These kept people from believing and trusting Him with childlike faith.

Satan presented Jesus with the very things that mattered most to him. He offered Jesus three very religious alternatives like miracles, mystery and authority. Jesus turned all three down. He just wanted to be the beloved son of His Father living a life of simple trusting obedience and return to Him with a bride bought and paid for.

Character determines *greatness*–the humility to become as trusting as children. (Matt. 18:3,4). This highway of humility leads into the likeness of an ever expanding universe of knowing God. Or it determines *failure*–trying to serve two masters.

" . . . for that which is highly esteemed among men is detestable in the sight of God."–Luke 16:15.

The rut of religious pride is to travel this trail of failure into the likeness of a deep black hole.

"Our iniquities, our secret heart and its sins [which we would so like to conceal from even ourselves], You have set in the [revealing] light of Your countenance"–Ps. 90:8 (AMP).

The Sufficiency of Grace
II Cor. 12:9
Out Of His Abundance

It is good for those who choose to leave the carnal and step through the gate of repentance—into all the provisions of God's righteousness and justice—to remember that for the rest of the journey, "grace is sufficient." Look back and see—there was "sufficient grace."

In Daniel 3:18, three men were about to be tossed into a furnace for not bowing down to a golden image of Nebuchadnezzar. They said, "Our God is able to deliver us . . . *but if not . . .* we are not going to serve your gods."

In Luke 24:21, two disciples on the road to Emmaus said to Jesus, *"But we were hoping* that it was He who was going to redeem Israel."

John the Baptist asks, *"are you the one,* or do we look for another?" Jonah in 4:2 (NKJV) complained "Ah Lord, w*as this not what I said* when I was still in my country? . . . for I know that you are a gracious and merciful God, slow to anger and abundant in lovingkindness . . ."

There are times in our lives when we have great expectations. Many, if not most are not realized the way they're imagined or feared or expected. When we fear opposition, it may not come. When we can't imagine why there should be opposition, it comes.

It is very important that faith has an alternative to present expectations. Like the three friends of Daniel saying "But even if He does not, let it be known to you, O king, that we are not going to serve your gods or worship the golden image that you have set up" (Dan. 3:18).

Anyone who grows in knowledge and faith will find Jesus contradicting their own ideas or expectations.

Since we all know only in part, we all will need to be brought into His holy purposes. He has notified us that His ways and thoughts are higher than ours. *His alternative will test the quality of our faith*. For many, disappointment becomes disbelief.

When the three men stood before the furnace, they did not know that God would do a far greater thing than they expected.

He joined them in the furnace and then demonstrated His grace and power to change a king's heart and mind.

When Abraham took Isaac to Mount Moriah, he did not know how or if God would provide another lamb for the sacrifice (Gen. 22).

Abraham's faith was faced with a serious question. If God does not provide a lamb other than Isaac, will I carry out this order? We read of him only that he rises early in the morning and arrives on the third day to make his offering, and becomes there a blessing to all future generations to come.

God joined himself to Jonah's preaching, and 600,000 people changed how they lived. Yet God was not living up to Jonah's expectations, and Jonah decided it was better to be angry at God and die. But did he know his experience in the whale foreshadowed Christ's death? That Jesus also was sent to a lost world to bring salvation to the nations?

Job was a man who lost everything and responded by saying, "Though He slay me, I will hope in Him" (Job 13:15). This was long before Lazarus was raised from the dead and Jesus was raised. Are we not all dead in trespasses and sin, waiting for a resurrection day?

Job was accustomed to having his sins forgiven (Job 7:21), but *one day God changed the format* of how he came to Job.

Job's willingness to suffer left a lasting testimony of a suffering Savior for generations to come. Of Him it was prophesied that, "His appearance was marred more than any man, and His form more than the sons of man. Thus will he sprinkle many nations" (Isa. 52:14).

How contrary this was to Israel's expectations. And because they had no alternative to their expectations, they said "Crucify Him!"

John the Baptist had seen the Holy Spirit in the form of a dove. He had heard the voice from heaven. Yet he asked "Are You the Expected One, or do we look for some one else?" (Luke 7:19).

How *different was jail to the Judean wilderness*, and Jesus to his expectation of what Israel's Messiah should do? Had John's flesh found something to argue about with his faith? It is possible to be a prophet of God and not understand the heart of God that delights in mercy.

Paul had enjoyed marvelous revelations and then received a thorn in his flesh. He asked three times for it to be removed. God's answer was "My grace is sufficient for you." (While you wait to understand). Why would God, who performed miracles through Paul, opened prison doors for him and *"disarmed rulers and authorities and made a public display of them"* (Col. 2:15), not remove a thorn from Paul's flesh? (II Cor. 12:7).

Paul needed to learn an alternative to his expectations.

> "Therefore I am well content with weaknesses, with insults, with distresses, with persecutions, with difficulties, for Christ's sake; for when I am weak, then I am strong."–II Cor. 12:10.

On our journey through the tabernacle, we, too, may need to learn and *accept God's alternatives to our expectations.*

Here is how Isaiah prophesies Jesus would face His own insults and distress and persecution. "Therefore I have set my face like flint (to live by faith) and I know I shall not be ashamed" (Isa. 50:7).

In Rev. 5:5, we read that one of the elders said to John, "stop weeping; behold the Lion that is from the Tribe of Judah, the root of David, *has overcome* so as to open the book and its seven seals."

This Redeemer now leads and intercedes to make us over comers.

My Redeemer
(Go'el in Hebrew)
Message of The Gospel

As we approach the altar, we need to be familiar with the Hebrew word *go'el*. It is very similar to our English word *gospel*. *Go'el* means *redeemer* and *gospel* is the *story of redemption*.

The first occasion for the use of this word was when Jacob blessed the sons of Joseph in Gen 48:15. "The angel who has *redeemed* me from all evil."

Job, who lived probably before or around the time of Abraham, uses the same word. "I know that my *Redeemer* lives" (Job 19:25).

Isaiah uses the term for the coming Messiah to Israel in Isa. 59:20: "A *Redeemer* will come to Zion."

In Prov. 23:11, the wise teacher has a warning; "For their *Redeemer* is strong," referring to God being the near kinsman who will protect the interest of the family.

The Hebrew word *Go'el* describes a person as a savior, a near relative, one who delivers, one who restores, one who puts something back into its original condition. God will do that with His creation someday.

It was also used of people who were next of kin who intervened to maintain the rights or preserve the continuity of the family.

The responsibility of a Go'el could involve:

Avenging the blood (life) of a murdered family member; redeeming someone from bondage or slavery; regaining family property to keep it in the family inheritance; or marrying a widow to provide an heir for her deceased husband, which was the case in the story of Ruth.

In Ex. 6:6, God calls Himself the *Redeemer*. "I will also redeem you with an outstretched arm." He promised to deliver them from bondage in Egypt and take them as His people to be their God.

This meant God not only had to get *Israel out of slavery in Egypt,* but in order to redeem, He would have to get *Egypt (sin in typology) out the hearts of Israel* and restore Israel to pristine, original, sinless condition.

This has been a work in progress for a long time, since the day of Adam and Eve. The means to accomplish this had been foreshadowed in offerings and sacrifices, in tabernacle and temple. Then in Jerusalem it was fulfilled and has been finished for 2000 years, but the application of this redemption to the ends of the earth is still in progress.

As we approach the altar of sacrifice, we will gain some insight into the means God provided for man to be redeemed. Understanding the sacrifices is very enabling and helpful to walk with God and with peace abide in Him as He abides in us.

Jesus reminded two men on the road to Emmaus of all that the prophets had spoken in Luke 24:26. "Was it not necessary for the *Christ to suffer* these things and *to enter into His glory*."

Hebrews 1:3 mentions those two things in different words: first, "when He had made purification of sins." This speaks of His ministry of humiliation and sufferings as the Lamb of God. This is the work of Jesus after the order of Aaron as high priest here on earth; and second, "He sat down at the right hand of the Majesty on High." This speaks of His ministry in power and glory as intercessor and King of Kings. It is the work of Jesus after the order of Melchizidek in heaven.

The first of these two parts was presented at the altar in the five different offerings, which pointed to the Redeemer's ministry of humiliation and suffering. The second part is seen in the holy place.

The New Testament writers testify of this redemption in various books:

As complete–we are working it out and begin to understand it
by obedience (Col. 2:10).

As effective–makes us a delight to God (Jude 1:24).

As experienced–a new kind of life flows out of them (Acts 4:31).

As for the universe–there will be a new heaven and earth and
humanity (Rev. 21:1,2).

As not worked for–it is worked upon (Phil. 2:12).

As an act of God–we must build our faith upon it (Acts 4:12).

As bringing the Holy Spirit–revealing the work of Christ (John 16:13).

As enabling us to become holy–and not just to have some pretty
ideas about God (Heb. 9:14).

As making us debtors to every man–until they know Him. (Matt.28:19).

As finished–it is the last word in the redemption of man.
It cannot be upset. The Redeemer's work brings
an end to spiritual pride and resistance in the
minds of people whose reasoning is opposed
to God's own testimony (Rev. 22:13).

It is the pride of one's own intelligence that loves to have preeminence over others. This pride exalts itself as the wisdom of man, while it holds other people in contempt. It blinds us to the magnitude of our own faults.

It despises the thought of being in need of God or His grace while one's own life degenerates into the spiritual conceit of worshipping idols.

It leads one to value spiritual ritual and tradition above fellowship, and forces God to ignore one's prayers.

We don't need to live like this. Humility is a far greater friend than pride ever can be. The Redeemer's work is not to bring an end to all things, only the end of one's old life.

The Altar of Sacrifice

Ex. 27:1–8
Made Him To Be Sin
II Cor. 5:21

The altar scene was not a pretty sight after coming through the attractive gate. Past the altar, one could see another attractive entrance into the tent of the presence. It was half as wide but twice as high.

But first, one must stop by this altar and let it make its contribution to a changed life. This had its beginning when God came looking for sinful man. And then drawn by grace through faith, entry was made through the gate.

As the gate was a type of the Redeemer, so also is this altar. The *gate invited everyone to come and enter into the righteousness of their Redeemer* " . . . through the foolishness of the message preached to save those who believe" (I Cor. 1:21). In redemption, "the foolishness of God is wiser than men, and the weakness of God is stronger than men" (I Cor.1:25).

The *altar was a revelation of the complete work of their Redeemer to secure this redemption*. It points to and speaks of the cross. It was to help people understand what man needed and what God required of them to restore peace between them.

He knew that leading an entire nation from slavery in Egypt and setting them on a journey to a promised land did in itself not change any human heart. It may have affected the thinking of some, but even a gift of that proportion cannot change a human heart to seek after God. "With most of them God was not well - pleased" (I Cor. 10:5). "It was not united with faith in those who heard" (Heb. 4:2).

So He set before Israel the things hoped for and needed in a three dimensional, illustrated form called typology. He wanted the people of Israel to understand their redemption full and free.

Where the law could only accuse and say "*guilty*," here at the altar, *grace was full and free to pardon*. God did not want Israel to add anything to it except applied faith. This alone enabled the observer to please Him and understand that God alone could remedy the sin issue. They were not to even think about adding a few good works to this justification to make sure.

For 1400 years this illustration of the complete work of their Redeemer was before them, and they kept putting faith in the keeping of the ceremonies instead of the one it pointed to. "It is these that bear witness of Me" (John 5:39). This Jesus was to be the true altar, capable of dying, and at the same time be the One upon whom the death penalty had no claim.

In Ex. 27, we find the description of the *bronze altar,* where the Redeemer was made to be sin.

It was *a square box*, open at the top and bottom, with dimensions of 5 by 5 by 3 cubits, or about 2.5 by 2.5 by 1.5 meters. Its sides were *acacia wood*, covered by *bronze inside and out*. The bottom half was *reinforced by a bronze grating* on the outside, halfway up to *a ledge around the middle* of the altar for the priest to stand on (Ex 27:5). The inside was *filled with earth and stones* (Ex. 20:24). At the upper four corners were *horns* pointing to the ends of the earth.

The acacia wood used is said to be from a bush-like tree with very crooked branches no more than 5–6 meters high. The wood is very hard and durable and described by the Greek translators as incorruptible. Here it speaks of the same humanity of Christ, as the poles of the court. Incorruptible and sinless, and not subject to death or decay, yet He could lay down His life.

This *wood was overlaid with bronze* pointing to the capability of the Sin-bearer to endure the fiery judgments of God without being consumed. It pointed to His power to endure the cross. At this altar, the holiness and righteousness of God were seen together in His hatred for sin and His justice for punishing it.

A. W. Pink writes in *Gleanings in Exodus*, "When Isaiah sees the holiness of God he cries out 'Woe is me, I am undone' (Isa. 6:5). He could not deal with his own sin, but he saw an altar and a live coal was taken from it. A coal that had done its work, it had consumed a sacrifice. This was applied to Isaiah's lips and he was declared clean. This live coal speaks of God's holiness consuming that which offends Him."

Peter writes of this consumed sacrifice in his first letter saying,

> " . . . you were not redeemed with perishable things like silver or gold from your futile way of life inherited from your forefathers, but with precious blood, as of a lamb unblemished and spotless, the blood of Christ. For He was foreknown before the foundation of the world, but has appeared in these last times for the sake of you . . ."–I Pet. 1:18–20.

The *four horns* were a symbol of strength pointing to the unfailing purpose of the Redeemer to finish His work on the cross. Though it was adequate for the whole world, it was applied to those who come by faith.

The dimension of *five cubits* speaks to us of grace, and it being *square* speaks of its equal application to people from every nation.

The *ashes* speak of the thoroughness of the fire's work. "It completely consumed the sacrifice and thereby declared the acceptance of the offerer by God," writes A. W. Pink.

The value of the heave offering was enormous. There was about 1.25 tons of gold, more than 5 tons of sliver and about 4 tons of bronze. Added to all these tons of metal were the precious stones, incense, spices, oil, acacia wood and then all the materials for curtains and coverings. But all the combined value of these could never redeem. There needed to be a life of substitution to redeem from sin.

In the blood there is not just a cancellation of sin, but payment in full. He who rejects the altar shuts himself out from the mercy of God. "Whoever touches the altar shall be most holy" (Ex. 29:37). The altar shows what God wants to do with the carnal flesh.

The Priesthood
Ex. 28:1
Holy And Royal

The reason for the altar is sin. The response is sanctification by participation, not just observation (Col. 3:16; I Cor. 12:14). One comes to the Redeemer as he is, but he dare not stay that way. Approaching the holy place does not happen until sin is dealt with.

There is no communion before cleansing (I Cor. 11:28). One needs to be willing for God to strangle in us the things that always make us pursue after our own point of view, our own interests, our own cleanness. A willingness for all these to be put to death gives the God of peace the open door to use us for His intended purposes.

Where there was an altar, there needed to be a priesthood. While *the altar secured* the relationship between God and the redeemed, *the priesthood was for maintaining* this relationship. The same grace that protected Israel at the Passover in Egypt was now at Mount Horeb, providing the means to keep them (I Pet. 1:5). As Israel *had a priesthood*, so the church *is a royal priesthood* with Jesus, as our high priest.

After God had through Moses laid out the order for coming *to* His people (Ex. 25:10–27:19), He begins laying out the requirements for what Israel was *to bring* into His presence (Ex. 27:20).

His first instruction to them is "to charge the sons of Israel that they bring you clear oil of beaten olives *to make a lamp burn continually.*"

"Aaron and His sons shall keep it in order from evening to morning before the Lord" (Ex. 27:21). It was the *first responsibility* of the priesthood.

God would look after His Shekinah glory in the most holy place inside the veil, but the *responsibility for light in the holy place* falls to the priesthood.

The first thing God provides for is light.

> " . . . God is light, and in Him there is no darkness at all."
> (I John 1:5)

It is man who "loved the darkness, rather than the light; for their deeds are evil" (John 3:19). They need to come to the light.

At creation, it was His first provision. "Let there be light" (Gen. 1:3). At Pentecost, the responsibility of keeping the light was given to the church, the royal priesthood of all believers.

They were to be *like wicks* in the lamp stand, soaking up the Holy Spirit (the oil). And with just enough of themselves exposed and trimmed, be the means by which the Holy Spirit could cast the light of God's glory before God and man.

Even in this place of privilege for the royal priesthood, they remember the words of Paul, "I find then the principle that evil is present in me, the one who wishes to do good" (Rom. 7:21).

The priesthood was (and is) to bear their guilt (Num. 18:1,23). They were responsible for the consequences of any defilement that came to the sanctuary or themselves. They were like parents who bear the responsibility for the things they or their children do. They were to instruct, discipline and judge, but also to mediate on behalf of them before the mercy seat of God, on the merits of the perfections of their Redeemer, not their own successes or failures.

In both Ex. 29 and Lev. 8, we are given a detailed description of their consecration and the inherent responsibility in their work.

The name *Aaron* means *very high*. He was given a place over all Israel; a type of Jesus "whom God exalted," (Acts 5:31), and who is called "great high priest" in Heb 4:14. This is a name which is used of no one else, not even Melchizidek. He is a type of the resurrected Christ who will come again to reign as King of Kings over all.

The high priest had two sets of clothes provided.

"In Lev.16, is mentioned what he wore on the annual Day of Atonement. Then he was robed in spotless white, foreshadowing the personal righteousness and holiness of the Lord Jesus, which fitted Him to undertake the stupendous work of putting away the sins of His people," writes A.W. Pink in his book "Gleanings in Exodus"

In Ex. 28, his official garments as high priest are described, pointing to the many attributes and perfections, which established his fitness for office. They were for glory and beauty, giving dignity to him and his work. "They pointed to Christ in all His perfections with the Father," writes A.W. Pink.

This Jesus as our high priest is very different from the covering cherub whose heart was lifted up because of his beauty. The prophets of old had described his downfall from his place of privilege around God's throne, to his disguise here on earth as king of Tyre and Babylon and in a multitude of other ways and places. Priestly mediation to redeem has never been a part of his agenda. Of the king of Tyre Ezekiel writes:

> "You had the seal of perfection, full of wisdom and perfect
> in beauty. . . . You were the anointed cherub who covers,
> and I placed you there. . . . And you sinned; therefore I
> have cast you as profane from the mountain of God. And I

have destroyed you, . . .Your heart was lifted up because of your beauty;You corrupted your wisdom by reason of your splendor."–Eze. 28:12–17.

The king of Tyre was not the only one inspired by Satan. Babylon also has had its inspiration from him. Isaiah writes of his ambitions in Is. 14:12–14:

> "How you have fallen from heaven O Star of the morning, . . . you said in your heart, I will ascend to heaven. I will raise my throne above the stars of God. I will sit on the mount of assembly . . . I will ascent above the height of the clouds. I will make myself like the Most High."

Multitudes are still under the influence, inspiration and control of these kingdoms of Babylon and Tyre. They specialize in encouraging man in the "I will's" of his pride to exalt himself and have preeminence above all others.

What praise, the redeemed can give to God for our great high priest who came in humility to mediate and satisfy the holy perfections of His Father and the needs of sinful man.

The Garments

Ex. 28

Perfections of His Character

The description given of the garments for Aaron's sons is very brief.

> "And for Aaron's sons you shall make tunics; You shall also make sashes for them, and you shall make caps for them for glory and for beauty. . . . And you shall make for them linen breeches to cover their bare flesh; . . . they made tunics of finely woven linen for Aaron and his sons.–.Ex 28:40–43; 39:27.

In 28:41, they are said to be for Aaron also, with the exception of the cap. The white linen here as elsewhere speaks of the pure holiness and righteousness of Christ.

On Aaron the high priest, the garments were far more elaborate. In type, the white linen of His righteousness was covered by all His other perfections, which are illustrated by the *robe of the ephod*, the *ephod*, the *onyx stones*, the *girdle*, the *breastplate*, the *turban*, and the *plate of gold*.

The robe of the ephod (Ex. 28:31–35) was a long, one-piece, loose blue garment over the white linen robe and under the ephod. It had openings for head and arms. Blue portrayed the heavenly character of the high priest. It's the first time the word *robe* is used in scripture and pertains to the high priest. It was a garment of dignity and gave priestly character to Aaron. It pointed to where our high priest is now.

Upon the hem were colored tassels like pomegranates. In

between each was a golden bell, "that its tinkling may be heard when he enters and leaves the holy place" (verse 34). The intercession of our high priest in heaven produced a sound at Pentecost, the fruit of which was 3000 saved (Acts 2:41) and adding daily (Acts 2:47; 5:14).

The ephod (Ex. 28:1) was of two pieces, covering front and back, joined over the shoulders by two straps and connected by the golden clasps that held the onyx stones. It was made of fine twisted linen, gold, blue, purple and scarlet material. The gold pointed to the divine glory of our high priest, the colors of His different perfections. The blue would point to Him as being from heaven above, the purple as Him being king and the scarlet as Him being the suffering servant of man kind.

Two onyx stones were set in gold on the shoulder straps. In Hebrew, onyx means to shine with luster. On them were engraved all the 12 names of the tribes by birth, testifying there was equal acceptance before God. The shoulder is a place of strength and speaks of their perfect security. Peter could testify to that by writing, "Who are kept by the power of God" (I Pet.1:5). Here they exhibit the likeness of God's people, where as on the breastplate they exhibited the diversity of God's people in their appointed gifts and glory.

The girdle was made of the same colors and linen, and was a symbol of service. Jesus did gird himself with a towel to wash the disciples' feet. He also promised that when He comes again, "He will gird himself . . . and will come up and wait on them" (Luke 12:37).

The breastplate (Ex. 28:15–30) was the most costly. The garments were background for it. It was made of fine twisted linen, doubled for strength, and was richly embroidered with the same three colors of the ephod.

Its size was ½ a cubit, or 22-25 cm. square. The bottom was

attached to the ephod by a blue ribbon through two rings, one on the breastplate and one on the ephod, the same on both sides. At the top, it was suspended by two gold chains attached to the gold clasps of the onyx stones on the shoulders.

It was the breast plate of judgment with the 12 names of the tribes inscribed on 12 gems, which Aaron carried into the holy place for a memorial before the Lord continually (verse 9).

The 12 gems may have been set in four rows of three along the edge of the breastplate, leaving the center free for *the Urim* (meaning *lights*) and *Thummin* (meaning *perfect rules*). "The law of the Lord is perfect" (Ps. 19:7) and the commandment of the Lord is pure, enlightening the eyes" (verse 8). The Urim and Thummin were a sign of the Lord being in the midst of Israel, wanting and ready to be consulted in times of need.

Israel was always *presented on the heart* of the high priest before God, expressing His affections for them. *Hanging from his shoulders,* it presents the strength and power of Christ engaged on behalf of His people. Their names could not be erased. *They were engraved* for lasting security. *They were secured* by gold and could not be lost. The power of God is chained to the tenderness of the heart of God. He is able to keep them from falling. Who will separate them from His love?

The twelve jewels represent His people who *are precious* in His sight. The gems *are durable* as is their salvation, which is purchased eternally.

The plate of pure gold was engraved with "Holiness to the Lord," and attached to the turban. It testifies that the high priest is holy, dedicated, undefiled and separate from sinners. As such, He interceded for them. It was God's provision for the imperfections and defilements of our service and worship. He bears the iniquities and presents His holiness on our behalf. In the perfections of Jesus our high priest is our eternal acceptance (Ex 28:38).

The turban speaks of His subordination to God and submission to His will. Only in one other place is the word for turban used (Eze. 21:25–27). There it speaks of the antichrist who has set himself up as God in the Temple of God. An event also mentioned in II Thes. 2:3–9.

At the time of the end, God says, "Remove the turban and take off the crown . . . Exalt that which is low and abase that which is high . . . until He comes whose right it is; and I shall give it to Him" (Eze. 21:25–27). To this Paul would add, " . . . who gave himself for our sin, that he might deliver us out of this present evil age" (Gal. 1:4).

Consecrate the Priesthood

Lev 8

Privilege And Responsibility

Jesus is recorded as praying in John 17:19, "*And for their sakes I sanctify myself, that they also may be sanctified by the truth.*" (NKJV) Jesus was saying, I give myself entirely to You as a holy sacrifice for them so they also might be entirely Yours, made holy by Your truth. He desires this for His people and provides the means to it.

The tabernacle and priesthood were a shadow of things to come. It is easier for a person who casts a shadow to understand what it represents than for someone who just sees the shadow. The one who casts the shadow is aware of three dimensions–of color, of depth, of feeling, of thought and of desire. The one who sees the shadow only sees a flat, two-dimensional image, often distorted by the direction of the light over the object of the shadow.

I think it is fair to say that God was presenting a great illustration at mount Horeb in order to convey more than just a flat, two-dimensional image of Himself. Why God chose to wait 1400 years to reveal Himself in the person of Jesus is not for me to answer. I am certain that faith was as much of an issue in the day of Moses as it was in Jesus day and is in our day.

Israel had less revelation of the Redeemer than the church does. The church will therefore be accountable for the whole revelation from Adam to the present. Jesus promised to the disciples that the Holy Spirit would come and "He shall take of Mine and shall disclose it to you" (John 16:14). He can also do that with what is revealed of Jesus in great detail in the Tabernacle. Four books of the Bible record the life of Jesus as the Son of Man here on earth. Sixty-two books reveal Him in other forms such as a prophet, priest, king, psalmist, apostle, pastor, evangelist, fisherman, carpenter, doctor, widow, mother, child, etc

To those who came to Him in faith, He was and is revealed "little by little" (Deut. 7:22). That has never changed. We are still instructed to "add to your faith" (II Pet. 1:5 NKJV). Consecration is required for this since it does not happen by wishful thinking.

From the story of Micah in Judges 17 and 18, it is evident that one does not have to go far from the revelation of Spirit and Truth at Shiloh to fabricate an entirely new religion absent of the faith required to know God. So when God consecrated the priesthood for Israel and the royal priesthood for the world, it was meant to *preserve the knowing and revealing of Himself* in a form that could be seen, practiced and understood.

The instructions God gives to Moses in Ex. 29 are being carried out in Lev. 8. There we read of the consecration for Aaron and his sons.

A.W. Pink mentions seven things in his book *Gleanings in Exodus* that Moses does for the Aaronic priesthood that Jesus now does for the royal priesthood:

> *They were taken from among the nation of Israel* (Lev. 8:2). God the Father chooses His elect out of Adam's race (Eph. 1:4).

> *They were brought to the door of the tabernacle* (Lev. 8:3). The called are brought to Christ (I Pet. 3:18).

> *They were washed all over with water from the laver* (Lev. 8:6). "He who has bathed needs only to have his feet washed" (John 13:10).

They were clothed in official garments (Lev. 8:7). "For all of you who were baptized into Christ have clothed yourself with Christ" (Gal. 3:27).

They were anointed with holy oil (Lev. 8:12). The Spirit of God is graciously anointing us for ministry (II Cor. 1:21).

Their hands were filled (Lev. 8:27). Signifying they were the Lord's in every faculty of their body soul, mind, feeling and strength. "Present your bodies a living and holy sacrifice to God" (Rom. 12:1).

They were consecrated to minister to God who would meet with them (Ex. 29:43, 44). All those who are believers, are "a holy priesthood" (I Pet. 2:5), and "a royal priesthood" (I Pet. 2:9).

"But to be a priest of God necessitates holy garments," writes A. W. Pink. We need to become familiar with being in God's presence. Our eternal life is to be spent there. We have the privilege of coming and abiding in His presence and serving in the holy place.

Moses called them, provided robes, washed them, clothed them and anointed them to the priesthood. He brought a bull for a sin offering so the priest would identify with the victim, and applied blood and oil for service and ministry.

He then presented the first ram as the burnt offering signifying their consecration to the priesthood. The *blood of the second ram* of ordination was put *on the tip of the right ear lobe*, signifying hearing from God; *on the right hand thumb*, signifying, doing the work of God; *and on the right foot big toe*, signifying walking in the ways of God. What remained was sprinkled on the altar, testifying to God's agreement. All this was provided for them as it is for us in Jesus Christ.

The responsibilities of Aaron and sons were to:

Put their hands on the sin offering (bullock) for substitution (Lev. 8:14).

Put their hands on the head of the first ram as burnt offering for consecration (Lev. 8:18).

Put their consecrated hands on the head of the second ram for ordination so as to speak with authority on behalf of God (Lev. 8:22).

Eat the meat of the ram and show bread, as partakers of Christ who is the bread of life and food of His people (Lev. 8:31).

Much has been provided for us in our Redeemer. His request to us that we lean hard on Him and delight in Him is not difficult. "By Him therefore offer up the sacrifice of praise to God continually . . . giving thanks to His name" (Heb. 13:15).

The Burnt Offering

Lev. 1

Consecration of Self to God

The First Offering

The Hebrew meaning of burnt offering is *"that which goes up."* Here was a demonstration of the Redeemer satisfying all the requirements for holy perfection of the God of Israel. It illustrated the first and great commandment—you shall love the Lord your God with all your heart, soul, mind and strength. It was in type, *the complete consecration* of the Redeemer to fulfill the will and intended purpose of God. In satisfying God's need for holiness, He could meet man's need for redemption.

This kind of consecration is not found much among the masses who like big fast freeways to lead them to their destinations. It is often a narrow, lonely way of demonstrated love. We are called on to be holy at any cost. If obedience costs us our life, then lets pay it.

The offering was to be *a male without blemish*, representing the second Adam, who was without sin. It was to be presented *according to one's possession*. If a person owned a herd of cattle, he could not bring an offering from a flock of sheep, nor could he bring a pigeon or turtledove. These were for the offerings of the poor.

Each animal represents a different characteristic of the Redeemer. The *ox/bullock*, tells of His strength and patient endurance as Savior. The *sheep or lamb* speaks of Him as meek and gentle (Isa. 53:7). The *goat* speaks of Him as one chosen from the flock, and that this one dying saved the whole flock. . (John 11:5). The *dove and pigeon* speak of His peace and loving tenderness, His mourning and grieving innocence.

The offering was to be brought to "the doorway of the tent of meeting, that he may be accepted before the Lord" (Lev. 1:3). It was no longer to be done in the open field as before, because the blood (the life of the person it represented) was now to be presented before God in their midst, not before idols of other nations.

The offerer was to lay his hand on the head of the animal. In Hebrew it means to *lean hard*. "Your wrath lies heavy upon me" (Ps. 88:7 NKJV). It indicated *we identify with the victim*. Our faith leans on the same person God leaned His wrath on. It is the basis for a peaceful conscience.

The priest's work was to take the blood (which represented the life of the offerer) to the altar before God and sprinkle it around and upon the altar as evidence of atonement for all to see, but seen only by those who come near the altar. The Redeemer poured out His life blood for all to see. "Turn to Me and be saved . . ." (Isa. 45:22).

The priest was to skin only the ox/bullock to portray how defenseless the victim was without a covering. This was perhaps necessary for the rich and powerful like Jairus as head of a synagogue or the ruling Sanhedrin to see and feel this, reminding them that before God they were without cover. It was then cut in pieces for *complete exposure and examination* (Lev. 1:6), before the all-seeing eyes of God who is "able to judge the thoughts and intentions of the heart" (Heb. 4:12). The unblemished insides of the offering revealed there was no imperfection in the consecration of our Redeemer. The goat, sheep and lamb were not skinned, but cut in pieces for complete examination.

The Redeemer, being *without blemish*, satisfied the holy perfections of God and was therefore accepted in the place of the redeemed sinner. For the offerer, it was a graphic picture of identifying with the unblemished, innocent Redeemer, dying for the guilty. It was illustrated quite clearly that the Redeemer received it from both ends. *First, the sinner leans hard* his need and dependence on his substitute, and *then God's wrath was poured out* on Him until he was completely consumed.

The head on the altar tells of the mind of the Redeemer who leaned on His Father (Lev. 1:8). He did not lean on His own understanding (Prov. 3:5). *The fat* speaks of His devotion and affection (Lev. 1:8), which belonged only to God. *The insides without defect* speak of no inner defilement in His will, mercy and purity (Lev. 1:9). *The legs* speak of His *outward* walk not contaminated by other attractions (Lev. 1:9). He knew no sin (II Cor. 5:21), and He was without sin.

The dove and pigeon had *the head wrung off* to indicate the violence done to the Redeemer. *The crop removed* meant to say He offered up no sinful appetites. *Removing the feathers* tells of a covering removed to expose one's true self. *The tearing of the wings* speaks of no way of escape (Lev. 1:14–16).

It was an offering by fire, a soothing aroma to the Lord because it represented the Redeemer in His perfections and devotion to the Father's will. *This fire was never to go out* (Lev. 6:13). Every Israelite could see this fire consume its victim on their behalf all day and night long, a testimony to God's hatred of sin, but also to the way of escape from its judgment.

This all-consuming fire was not user-friendly or seeker-sensitive. For there will always be enough fuel in hell to satisfy the justice of God. And this justice will never fail to find sufficient satisfaction in the life of the redeemer to offer pardon. Here for all to see was put on display *the consecration of the son to the Father.*

The ashes were evidence that the victim had been consumed by fire. The ashes were removed from the altar by the priest in his linen robes, for everything that had touched the altar was holy. In another robe, he carried them outside the camp to a clean place

(Lev. 6:11; Eze. 44:19). Jesus also was taken outside of Jerusalem and, having been made sin, was put in the new tomb of Joseph (a clean place), from which he arose to cleanse a people for himself from every nation.

Death of Consecration

I Kings 13

Please Read the Story

I Kings 12:25–13:32

The burnt offering illustrates pure and complete consecration.
The following three chapters illustrate faulty consecration.

After a short time on his father Solomon's throne, Rehoboam loses the northern tribes of Israel to Jeroboam, who in turn after a few years, fears losing his throne back to Rehoboam due to the temple being in Jerusalem.

He decides to build two altars of Baal with golden calves and places one of them in the city of Dan in the north and the other in the city of Bethel in the south. His reason for building them was, "it is too much for you to go to Jerusalem; behold your gods, oh Israel that has brought you up from Egypt" (I Kings 12:28). So idol worship was officially inaugurated in Bethel.

There lived in this town of Bethel an old prophet. It appears he had settled down into inactivity. Perhaps because of aging, but it seems from the recorded story that he had a score to settle with God.

Maybe he felt like Jonah up on the mountain, who thought he had good reason to get angry at God while he was waiting for the end of Nineveh, an event that did not take place because the people of the city repented.

We do know the old prophet was not at the inauguration. His sons were. We don't know how long he had been silent, but we read that a prophet from Judah (I'll call him young prophet) was sent to speak against this altar and its idol worship.

Were the sons at the feast because they were not following the God of their father? Or were they excited about the new way they could now worship God? Did the sons realize that their father should have been there to speak against the altar? We don't know.

They did report on the events of the day. The young prophet had foretold that the priests of the high places would be sacrificed on their altars by a descendant of king David named Josiah. This prophesied event occurred some 300 years later (II Kings 23:20). He also said the altar would split apart, which it did at that very moment, and then at the king's command to seize the prophet, his arm seized.

When the old prophet heard this, he was no longer silent.

Up to this point in the story, one could ask if *consecration had died in him* before he did. Was he tired perhaps of being called an old prophet?

Did he remember that insubordination to God is as the sin of iniquity and idolatry (I Sam. 15:23), and very much in contrast to consecration?

Was his silence the sin of iniquity? *Had he quenched the Spirit* in years past? Had he become insubordinate to the voice of God and therefore silent towards idolatry?

Had pride (self-preservation) silenced him to Jeroboam's sin and made him a liar to the prophet of Judah? Why did he lie about eating bread and drinking water? Was he jealous of God's instant confirmation of what the young prophet had spoken? Had he wanted to see God's instant confirmation of what he had spoken in the past without seeing any? Was he angry at God for not having had an alternative to his expectations of what God should do?

Was the victim of the old prophet any less a victim than those of Jeroboam of whom it is said, "He made Israel sin" (I Kings

14:16)? And then there were the victims of Balaam of whom it was said, "He caused Israel to trespass" (Num. 31:16)?

The same *weapon of prophesy* he had used to speak for God; he now used to kill a man of God–the young prophet. He blended it with friendliness, a touch of authority and a suggestion of divine guidance.

I think he may have used it that way before and lost his ministry. *He now succeeded in killing someone else's purpose to obey God.*

The confirming evidence of the split altar and the seizing of the king's arm yielded in the young prophet to the lie of the old prophet. He had obeyed the first half of his instruction. He then disobeyed the second half. The *consecration* of the young prophet yielded to deception of the old prophet.

The tragedy that crowned the old prophet's success was the death of the young prophet. Therefore y*ou cannot measure consecration by success,* financial or otherwise. Watch out what you applaud!

Now the story takes and unexpected turn. The amazing grace of God can bring an event that will reactivate or resurrect the consecration that has died in us. For "The Word of the Lord came" (I Kings 13:20) and the old prophet prophesied again. It is as the apostle Paul says, "the gifts and the calling of God are irrevocable" (Rom. 11:29). These are ours for the duration of our life to use in ministry to others.

Though there was no apparent repentance in Israel or its king, it appears that the *event was for the sake of God's grace to be shown* to the old prophet, to lead him to repentance and mourn. (I Kings 13:29).

The grace of God appears to us much more than we give God credit for. "The grace of God has appeared to all men, *teaching us . . ."* (Titus 2:12). This means that although grace appears to all men, it can only teach those who in the events of their life recognize in these the grace of God appearing to them, like

King Josiah (II Kings 23:15–20), or Jairus did by falling at Jesus feet (Mark 5:22).

Everything the old prophet knew he should have been, the younger prophet was. The old prophet wanted to be and was buried in the same grave as the young prophet from Judah.

The *gift of God* (the ministry or service) *can only reveal* what is in our hearts. The gift cannot change the heart, even though it can bless others.

It is one's consecration to trust what God has said *that will change the heart* and transform it into Christ likeness.

Defective Consecration
I Sam. 15
Selective Obedience

From Israel's first encounter with Amelek, God had declared the memory of them would be blotted out from under heaven (Ex. 17:14).

While Saul was king over Israel, this termination was to be enacted. As king, Saul had acted valiantly and established Israel as a nation with a standing army. He knew how to give orders and demand obedience.

He had also demonstrated that he himself was not always obedient (I Sam. 13:9). Saul was quite willing to be king over Israel, but being servant and subject to God gave him some difficulties. Consecration is to be a servant that crowns God as Lord of all.

After defeating Amelek, Saul had all the appearance of success. But while Israel was celebrating, God was grieving. Saul had three priorities ahead of consecration.

He wanted to be remembered (I Sam. 15:12), for his success, so his pride builds a statue on Mt. Carmel, hoping it would be there long after his death.

He tells a half truth (verse 13), hoping God would be as pleased as he was, but knowing the other half was unfit (blemished) to be a burnt offering.

He blames the people (verse 21). He would rather give them what they want and so have their approval of him, than have God's blessing.

A true sacrifice of praise needs no applause. *To a consecrated heart, applause is cheap.* It is quite possible to say, "Blessed are you of the Lord" (verse 13) to Samuel or anyone else, while sheep are bleating behind you. These sheep told the truth about Saul and us. Defective consecration always has some sheep bleating behind it. It says, "God's grace is not sufficient for me."

Samuel answers Saul, "Wait," (verse16), or be still. As God, he knows things about your desperately wicked heart that you don't. "I, the Lord, search the heart, I test the mind . . ." (Jer. 17:10).

So why not obey the voice of God until Amelek is destroyed in us. In our every act of obedience, we, too, have opportunity to keep some bleating sheep for ourselves. We know how to blame others, tell half truths, and build statues so others will remember us. How deceptive is the victory over other people or causes when it exposes our own defective consecration.

Saul was to utterly destroy Amelek. Amelek was to utterly destroy in Saul all double-minded ideas of obedience.

Defective consecration is very selective in choosing what to remember of all that God has said. Instead " . . . you shall remember all the way the Lord your God has led you . . . that He might humble you, testing you to know what was in your heart, whether you would keep His commandments or not" (Deut. 8:2).

Counterfeit Consecration
Judges 17–18
Manmade Ministries

In the hill country of Ephraim in the vicinity of the tabernacle, there lived a man named Micah, which means, "Who is like unto Jehovah."

His mother had given him a good name, but there were other things she left him that were not good. Her uncontrolled tongue was one. "For with it we bless our Lord and Father and with it we curse men" (Jam. 3:9).

The mother finds 1100 pieces of her silver missing (about 34 lbs.) and pronounces a curse on the thief. Micah overhears this and ponders his future.

Perhaps he had heard and remembered enough from his forefathers of the blessings and curses that would come to those who kept or broke the law. He now fears for his life and decides it is better to confess to his mother than live under a curse.

The mother is delighted and dedicates the silver to the Lord by turning it into graven and molten images for her son. She also has a very selective memory of the law that said you shall not make for yourself graven images.

He puts them in a shrine, makes an ephod and other household idols and consecrates one of his sons to be a priest.

Then a Levite comes by, and Micah hires him to carry out the priestly functions. He concludes that "now the Lord will prosper me" (Jud. 17:13).

His thinking was a counterfeit peace offering. In his case, there was no leavened cake waved before the Lord (Lev. 7:14).

Counterfeit consecration necessitates manmade ministries and is therefore absent of grace and the possibility of knowing God. God gets put on the "honor" list of man. Almost everything is manmade—wealth, idols, priests, Levites, religion, ceremonies.

Then the Danites came through with 600 men of war (Judges 18). They took it all. Micah's gods are stolen from him.

If someone can steal from you the god you serve, it's an idol. Gods that can be stolen are not worth having.

With the Tabernacle so close by, how did all this idolatry happen? We read "In those days there was no king in Israel; every man did what was right in his own eyes" (Judges 17:6).

Idolatry is only possible when the inner throne of one's being is not filled with Christ as Lord and King.

Micah's mother gave him silver instead of herself. Gifts are not a substitute for personal consecration.

Counterfeit consecration can only bring further degeneration. It *cannot see "God's grace"* and therefore cannot be taught.

Grain/Meal Offering

Lev. 2:1–16

Consecrating gifts and ministry to others
The Second Offering

The altar of sacrifice was more than just a place where an animal once in a while died for someone's sin. There were five different offerings, each pointing to a different part of the complete work of redemption.

The first was the *burnt offering*. There we see the offerer gaining the acceptance of God by consecrating himself to love the Lord his God with all his heart, soul, mind and strength. As Jesus said, "This is *the first* and great commandment" (Matt. 22:38 NKJV).

The *grain offering* is like *the second commandment*. You shall love your neighbor as yourself (verse 39). Here the offerer consecrates his body and possessions to the Lord who has accepted him in the burnt offering. It was never offered apart from the burnt offering.

In the burnt offering, blood was used to express the life and soul of the offerer devoted to God.

In the grain offering, fine flour was used. The various presentations of flour shows in type the many circumstances and trials in which Jesus suffered and presented His life of ministry and service to man in obedience to God.

It expressed the various ways the offerer's body and possessions were devoted to God, to direct their use in ministry to others.

In the first offering, *everything was consumed* by fire and turned to ashes. In the second offering, *only a handful of flour*, mixed with oil and *all the frankincense* to express complete acceptance, was salted and put in the fire as a memorial of the complete grain offering (Lev. 2:2).

It brings the offerer into God's remembrance. In Acts 10:4, the "prayers and alms" of Cornelius are called a "memorial before God"

The remainder was eaten by the priests as unleavened cakes (Lev. 6:16). "I have given it as their share from my offerings by fire" (Lev. 6:17). God's concern was not only for His own glory, but also the needs of man.

The Hebrew word for this offering is Minchâw, meaning *a bloodless voluntary sacrificial offering or present.* An example of this is Jacob selecting a present for his brother (Gen. 32:13). It was a present meant to reflect how much the giver valued the recipient.

Like Jacob, Jesus brings his life of service and ministry to sinful humanity as a present to the recipient, His Father. He values His Father to the extent of being willing to be ground as grain into fine flour by much rejection, unbelief, pride, the garden of Gethsemane, and the cross.

In Lev. 2:1–7, the meal offering was to *be presented in one of three ways.* (When they arrived in Canaan, they could also bring it in the form of the heads of early ripened grain Lev. 2:14–16). The ingredients of flour, oil and incense were the same in all three, but the flour was presented differently. It was presented *according to the offerer's status* or means, as measured by whether they *had an oven, a grill, or a pan.*

They were to bring it as *fine wheat flour, sifted well of bran* (Lev. 2:1). It was to be *no less than an omer* (Lev. 6:20), about 5 pints or a day's food supply. Usually it was made into the form of 10 cakes or wafers, of which one was put in the fire of the altar. At the consecration of the tabernacle the leaders seem to have brought far more than an omer in a silver bowl, heaped full and mixed with oil, plus a gold pan full of incense (Num. 7:13–14).

The priest was to take a handful (or one of the cakes) of the offerer's flour to the altar (Lev. 6:15), whether he was rich or poor, and offer it to the Lord. Not having the problem of personal favoritism, God has never despised the poor or anyone not gifted greatly in the things and knowledge of Himself.

Grain offering brought as cakes baked in an oven (Lev. 2:4).

These ovens were common among the upper and middle class. The cakes were made of unleavened bread *mixed* with oil or unleavened wafers of smaller size *spread* with oil. Food cooked in an oven was well-prepared and processed. The offerer's life was to be in demonstration of this. God's holiness was to be *mixed* into their daily life and speech. Ministry to others was to be *spread* with His presence and Spirit.

Grain offering brought as cakes made on a fire plate (Lev. 2:5–6).

These were unleavened cakes *mixed* with oil, then *broken* in pieces and oil poured on them. Here is a life of holiness, but it is broken and problematic. Faith appears to be less mature, but life is yielded and made effective by the Holy Spirit poured upon it. Problems of poverty, illness, oppression, abuse, etc. are seen in the light of faith, forgiveness and prayer instead of anxiety and worry.

Grain offering brought as fine flour in a pan with oil (Lev. 2:7).

This was a shallow clay vessel that indicated poverty. Whatever our means of personal wealth are missing, the oil must be present. We must be born again. When we are, even teachers and leaders can at times be amazed at our fullness of understanding His life and kingdom (Luke 2:47). As we receive this new life from God, whether in riches or poverty, so we give it to God and man. We learn to apply His Word and promises as we receive them.

When we say, "Jesus is Lord," we cannot offer excuses in the place of our gifts and calling. In presenting 10 (number of responsibility) cakes, the offerer acknowledged his responsibility to love his neighbor as himself.

The Ingredients

Lev. 2, Lev. 6

Beautiful Standing Grain Ground as Fine Dust

In I Sam. 1:24, we can read the story of Hanna and Samuel, going to Shiloh to offer a burnt offering, a grain offering, and a libation offering. She brings 3 bullocks, 1 ephah of fine flour, and a jug of wine. This was enough for *three burnt offerings and ten grain offerings.*

Her prayer in I Sam. 2 would tell why. Here was a mother who made a vow (I Sam. 1:11), kept it, and rejoiced in it. So there were people in Israel who understood the significance of the offerings and what they pointed to and were glad to avail themselves of the provisions promised to them through these offerings.

When Hanna's prayer was ended, we read, "Now the Sons of Eli were worthless men; they did not know the Lord" (I Sam.2:12). In the next 22 verses, the entire household of Eli has its doom foretold. By chapter 4:17–18, Eli *lost the war* to the shame of Israel. *He lost his sons* to the shame of his household, *he lost his life* to his own shame, and *he lost the ark* to the shame of God. The *price of not listening to God is huge* and has eternal consequences. Their lives were disconnected from the typology that stood before them.

The titles and positions of Eli and his sons had brought added responsibility to them. They were to bear the iniquities of Israel before God as mediators (Lev. 10:17). But their positions before God and Israel were of no use to them in bringing a change to the condition of their own heart. It only revealed what was already in them. One can only imagine what blessings would have come to Israel had they all lived with a heart like Hanna, who brought an abundant grain offering.

The ingredients of *what we offer* and *how* we offer them to God is important. Take, for example, the Sabbath rest as an ingredient. "For we who have believed enter that rest" (Heb. 4:3). Verse 4 identifies this as the Sabbath rest. "And God rested on the 7th day from all His works."

Isaiah 58:13 records for us how to present this important rest as an ingredient in the grain offering. It is offered by " . . . desisting from *your own way,* from seeking *your own pleasure* and from speaking *your own words.*" The rest that comes from believing was not only meant for Israel. God's instruction to do it His way, seek His pleasure and speak His words will be in effect long after the resurrection and the church ceases to exist on earth.

While the meal offering was *voluntary* for the people, the high priest was *required* to present this offering *entirely* in the fire of the daily burnt offerings. He was required to bring 12 cakes to represent the 12 tribes.

Jesus *voluntarily* gave himself for the people of God (John 10:18), yet God *required* He offer Himself *entirely* on behalf of them (Luke 22:42).

The giving of ourselves to the service of man needs to reflect this.

The fine wheat flour was *very finely ground* and sifted well. In the flesh, we are like standing grain. Good to look at, but in order to be presented and made useful, we need to be ground like flour.

The flour speaks of Christ. *As the flour was ground, so Jesus was ground* by all the unbelief, rejection, hatred, pride and humiliation of others. To these were added the agony of His suffering in the garden of Gethsemane and at His trial and crucifixion. The

Father placed on Him the sin and judgment of the world and the hell of separation from Him. This was His gift of service to man. In Luke 20:18, Jesus warned that unless they would fall on Him, they themselves would be scattered like dust. That speaks of a severe grinding. All those who lean on Him would be broken of sin and pride and legalism and hypocrisy, while He would carry the wrath of God and experience the grinding for them.

The oil mixed in speaks of Jesus being "full of the Holy Spirit" (Luke 4:1). *The oil poured on* is spoken of by Isaiah in 11:2. "The Spirit of the Lord shall rest upon Him." It set Him apart for His work and office even as every king and priest was set apart.

Frankincense was the aroma of His life toward the Father. The fragrant smell meant the offering was acceptable to God.

There was to be no honey, which included all sweet things obtained from fruit. Three hundred pounds of dates and grapes could make 100lbs. of sweetener, called "dibs" in Arabic. It could turn sour and lead to fermentation. What we offer to God does not need to please us, but must be holy and separated from the carnal.

There was to be no leaven of selfish intent, malice, evil thought or grumbling because it indicates corruption at work. It puffs up. The things that speak of Christ must not have man's ideas added to them.

Jesus warns of the leaven of the Pharisees. In Luke 20 He speaks of their past rejection of the truth of John the Baptist (verses 3–8). This had swollen to their present rebellion against Him (verses 9–16), and would lead to their future ruin (verses 17–18).

"Every grain offering . . . you shall season with salt" (Lev. 2:13). Where leaven corrupts, salt preserves. A covenant with salt was an absolutely sure agreement. It was called "the salt of the covenant of your God" (Lev. 2:13). It speaks of friendship between God

and man and His unchanging satisfaction with our redeemer, but also our own truthful surrender to the Lord by which all impurity, ritual and hypocrisy are rejected.

Drink offerings were presented with the meal and peace offerings. It was added to express the worshipper's hearty agreement in all that was displayed at the altar.

Unintentional Sin

Lev. 4

Contentment with Sin
The Third Offering

Iniquity is a word used some 300 times in the Old Testament. It means perverted truth. It brings with it a contentment to live with things that God's righteousness will not. We may not feel hostile toward God, but for the most part are content with how we are.

Mankind has long had priorities very different from those that satisfy God's holiness. We are for the most part conscious and deliberate about what we do and think, but we do not see it as sin at the time.

Perhaps more sin is done in ignorance than sin in direct violation of our own conscience or in willful violation to another's conscience. We may be committing a sin similar to the angels that were cast out of heaven and into hell and be unaware or untroubled by it.

Sin is deceitful. Who can understand his errors? Only God knows how desperately wicked is the human heart. When He shines some of His light and truth upon us, then it brings to us an ability to see some of our ignorance. The truth enables us to see the condition of our hearts.

In Lev. 11–16, there are a series of chapters where God is casting some enlightenment on our ignorance by giving numerous examples about the existence or evidence of sin, the effect of sin, the discerning of sin, etc. He lives where holy perfection is normal. Those who don't think themselves ignorant should try to describe this perfection.

Try to describe someone who is everywhere present at the same time, past and future included, who speaks an entire universe into existence. If one doesn't think He did this, do you think there will be a resurrection? It will take place in the twinkling of an eye (I Cor. 15:52). Not unlike creation,

It did not take Lazarus long to come out of his grave when Jesus told him to come out. And the antichrist will not take long to obey the word of Jesus on his final day.

For this ignorance of man, God made a provision. His mercy and compassion for sinful man is such that *He instituted a sacrifice for the sin of ignorance.* It was for everyone from the high priest, to the entire nation. It was for the ruler and the common man as well as the very poorest among them.

No one is exempt from having the light of God's presence and word reveal "Our iniquities, our secret heart, and its sins [which we would so like to conceal even from ourselves]. You have set in the [revealing] light of your countenance" (Ps. 90:8 AMP).

When a person became guilty, he was to *bring an offering to the door of the tabernacle.* This was to prevent the establishment of other sacred sites and practices. In coming to the door, they were in effect coming to the foot of the cross, since both the encampment of the tribes of Israel and the tabernacle furniture were laid out in that form.

Here the offerer was to lay his hands on the head of the animal that *would be his substitute.* Here sin was reckoned over to the sin bearer, or as we now say, sin is imputed, or reckoned to Christ. Jesus our substitute became our sin bearer.

For the sin of a high priest (Lev. 4:3) or the sin of the entire nation (Lev. 4:13), the *animal was a bullock.* The bullock was most costly and visible to the eye. But it also speaks of the patient enduring strength of the sin bearer. Whether it is the high priest or whole nation, they equally needed to lean on this sin bearer. The sin of one is equally as serious as the other.

For the ruler or elder (Lev. 4:22), the offering was *a male goat*, most commonly used in the sin offering. The *common man* (Lev. 4:27) was required to bring a *female goat or lamb* without blemish. If he were *poor* (Lev. 5:7), he could bring *two pigeons, two turtledoves, or one omer of flour* (Lev. 5:11), which was a day's supply and would indicate a day's fast. The poor had far less means and responsibility for the direction of the nation.

Having leaned on the animal's head, the animal was slain and the blood was caught in a bowl. For the sin of the High priest and nation, it was *taken into the holy place* (Lev. 4:5). In its utter helplessness, the life of the offerer, represented by the blood in a bowl, is brought before God. It is the blood, *by reason of the life of Christ it represents,* that makes atonement.

The day did come when Jesus as "the Apostle and High Priest of our confession" (Heb. 3:1) brought His own blood through the veil and to the mercy seat in the heavenly tabernacle.

The priest was *to sprinkle it seven times on the ground* before the veil. Lev. 4:6. This represented the place of our perfect standing before God and completeness in Christ, implying God is fully satisfied.

Some blood was to be *put on the horns of the altar of incense* (Lev. 4:7). This altar speaks of Christ as intercessor. The horns are the symbol of power. *The fragrant incense* represented that which is pleasing and acceptable.

Here, the life of the Redeemer, represented by the blood, is identified with the power of Jesus as the great and pleasing intercessor before the Father. The remainder was poured at the altar of sacrifice as evidence that atonement was needed even for the high priest.

When a priest sinned, he sinned in the things of God. The

blood went in to the altar of intercession. The priest's work was to intercede, but he also *needed to be interceded for.*

For the ruler, elder, and common man, *the blood stayed outside* on the horns of the altar of sacrifice and at its base (Lev. .4:25) as *evidence for all Israel* to see that their own sin was also atoned for

The Exhibition of Blood

Lev. 6–7

Helpless Surrender; Abundant Benefits

The sin offering receives three times more coverage than each of the other four offerings. It even provides three examples illustrating specific areas of our ignorance in need of God's revealing light. These illustrations will come in a later chapter.

Have you thought about what was mentioned previously, how *ones life, being represented by the blood,* was carried in a bowl into the presence of God? Was there a more helpless way to be brought to Him? To be presented before God by a Redeemer who not only redeemed you but speaks for you on the basis of His own merits and perfect life and none of your own good works.

Your contribution was simply to come and trust this Redeemer and have faith in Him. For, " . . . my God shall supply all your needs according to His riches in glory in Christ Jesus" (Phil. .4:19).

One of the riches in glory is the great work of grace that the life and blood of Christ Jesus represented. No one but a person troubled and burdened by sin could relish the never varying exhibition of blood at the altar, because here is what God says it will do.

It brings forgiveness. It frees the guilty one from the burden of sin. " . . . through Him forgiveness of sin is proclaimed to you" (Acts 13:38).

It brings redemption. It is freely given and cannot be bought. "In Him we have redemption through His blood, the forgiveness of our trespasses according to the riches of His grace" (Eph. 1:7).

It brings cleansing. There is a cleansing for all those defiled by their sinful past from its shame and dominion. " . . . if we walk in the light as He Himself is in the light, we have fellowship with one another, and the blood of Jesus His Son cleanses us from all sin" (I John 1:7).

It brings justification. This protects the accused one from the penalty of sin. "Much more then, having been justified by His blood, we shall be saved from the wrath of God through Him" (Rom. 5:9).

It brings sanctification. No need to make any attempt at redemption through good works. "Therefore Jesus also, that He might sanctify the people through His own blood, suffered outside the gate" (Heb. 13:12).

It brings peace with God. The formerly alienated and hostile are now reconciled. " . . . it was the Fathers good pleasure . . . through Him to reconcile all things to Himself, having made peace through the blood of His cross" (Col. 1:19,20).

It brings access to God. " . . . you who were far off have been brought near by the blood of Christ" (Eph. 2:13).

Imputation

Rom. 5:18

To Reckon Over to One's Account

For all these benefits to be of any use to me, there had to be a way to apply them. If I cannot earn them or deserve them, then God would have to impute them, meaning *to reckon it over to one's account.*

Paul, in Rom. 5:12–21, explains how this works.

First he contrasts *Adam's offense* to Christ's free gift (verse 12). Next he contrasts *the effects of sin* to Christ's free gift (verse 16). Then he contrasts *the two reigns* of death and life (verse 17). He finishes by comparing the *two acts of transgression and righteousness.* " . . . through one transgression, there resulted condemnation to all men." It was *imputed to them.* "Even so, through one act of righteousness, there resulted justification of life to all men." (verse 18). It also was *imputed to them.*

When one is born again of the Spirit and baptized into Christ's death and raised with Him to a new life, then Christ's righteousness becomes the believer's by a legal endowment. This righteousness of God is then imputed to the believer, and it becomes his forever by a judicial act.

> "But by His doing you are in Christ Jesus, who became to us wisdom from God, and righteousness and sanctification and redemption"–I Cor. 1:30.

Christ is made to the believer the righteousness from God.

To the Roman church Paul writes:

"Being justified as a gift by His grace, through the redemption which is in Christ Jesus, whom God displayed publicly as propitiation in His blood through faith"–Rom. 3:24–25.

Propitiation is the act through which Jesus gained our forgiveness and God's favor. For by one offering He has perfected for all time those who are sanctified (Heb.10:14).

In Ps. 103:6 we read, "He made known His ways to Moses and His acts to the people of Israel." I think Moses understood quite clearly what we call imputation and propitiation. The responsibility of the priesthood was to teach this to the nation.

I know that hindsight is clearer than foresight, but I believe that God making "known His acts to the people of Israel" Ps. 103:6, is no different than God making known the Acts of the Apostles to the church.

Think how they repented (Acts 2:37), were baptized (verse 41), were devoted to teaching, communion and prayer (verse 42), had all things in common (verse 44), and had no written New Testament.

The foolishness of the tabernacle is no different than the foolishness of the cross, Christ, and Christ crucified. It was and is and will be the wisdom of God in an apparently foolish package.

Unintentional Sin—Continued
Lev. 5:1–4 Three Examples
The Way The Truth The Life

Isaiah describes in part the work of the altar this way in Isa. 53:6:

> *"The Lord has caused the iniquity of us all to fall on Him."*

Paul describes what the altar illustrated in part in II Cor. 5:21.

> *"He made Him who knew no sin to be sin on our behalf"*

After the blood had been properly displayed and poured out, the priest had to remove all the *fat, two kidneys and liver from the bull* to offer them on the altar just as it was done in the peace offering. It was a sign of reconciliation and to show that *the offerer had been accepted* and that "they shall be forgiven" (Lev. 4:20).

If the *high priest* sinned against the holy things of God or if he caused others to sin, or if *Israel* as a nation sinned by worshipping idols or by grumbling against God, then the hide and the remainder of the bull was brought *outside the camp* to a clean place and burned with fire (Lev. 4:12).

The people are first shown pardon for their sin at the altar and then led outside the camp to see what God in judgment will do with it. Only the forgiven man is capable of seeing the horror of sin. "None but a pardoned man could have spoken Paul's cry; 'O wretched man that I am! Who shall deliver me from the body of this death' (Rom. 7:24)," wrote Andrew Bonar in his book *Leviticus*.

It was called *a clean place* because the ashes of all the other offerings brought into God's presence had been judged by a consuming fire on the altar and, having satisfied God, were brought to the clean place (Lev. 6:10–11). The ashes were later mixed in water for purification ceremonies (Num. 19).

On the evidence of the ashes that a holy, just and righteous God had been satisfied by an offering in His presence, sin is now judged outside the camp by the fire of His wrath in the presence of the whole congregation. "As if the altar were too near to God's presence to express what a sinner deserves in suffering torment far from God, all this was to be done outside the camp," wrote Andrew Bonar in his book Leviticus. "Therefore Jesus also, that He might sanctify the people through His blood, suffered outside the gate" (Heb. 13:12).

When *a ruler or common man* sinned, they were to bring *a male or female goat,* and the priest was to offer up its fat (Lev. 4:26), and boil its meat (Lev. 6:28) and eat it near the altar as evidence that the sinner was forgiven.

If it was boiled in an earthen pot, it was to be broken and not used again. The porous clay had absorbed the contamination of sin. Earth also has been contaminated by sin and will be broken and replaced with a new earth.

If it was boiled in a bronze vessel, then the vessel must be scoured to restore its ability to reflect the image of sinless perfection that once revealed the glory of God (Lev. 6:28).

Of *the two pigeons or doves* in Lev. 5:7, the first was offered for a sin offering. There was little from this little bird for the priest to eat to demonstrate acceptance, so the second bird was offered as a burnt offering to demonstrate complete acceptance by God Himself. The poorest could *bring an ephah of flour,* indicating a day's fast (Lev. 5:11).

One fire consumed all the 5 different sacrifices and offerings; a fire that was never to go out day or night. The whole camp could see this fire as a reminder of an everlasting fire of judgment for all who would not come.

But Israel was also aware that there was a victim on this altar, a substitute upon which God Himself looked with satisfaction. There His love and justice met together, and was made visible for all to see.

Three examples are given for God's people that required a sin offering.

To Adjure

This is to prevent the concealing of truth (Lev. 5:1). The judge in court was permitted to elicit information from a witness by solemnly charging (to adjure) him to answer and tell all he knew (Matt 26:63). If he omitted things he could have told or embellished them or misstated information he would be guilty of the sin of concealing the truth. The contrast is *to speak the truth*. As Jesus said, "I tell you the truth" (Luke 4:25).

Defilement

This is the sin of touching any unclean thing (Lev. 5:3), like the carcass of a dead beast, cattle, swarming things, or human uncleanness like leprosy, sores, boils, and much of our present media's enticement to pleasure, lust, covet, boast, etc. These blind us to the truth about ourselves.

Any degree of pollution was offensive to a holy God. Sin is the transgression of God's holiness, not our conscience. Though, "it is hidden from him . . . he will be guilty." The contrast to defilement is discernment of the unclean or the *discerning of truth.* As Jesus did by, "knowing what they were thinking in their heart" (Luke 9:47).

To Swear Thoughtlessly

This is the sin of making of a rash vow (Lev. 5:4). There is an overflow of hidden sin in our promises and resolutions and dedications expressed to God in prayer and song and practices. The contrast is to do what you say or sing, or in other words, *to practice the truth.* "Whatever the Father does, these things the Son does also in like manner" (John 5:19).

When Jesus said *"I am the way,"* He was speaking the truth. In saying, *"I am the truth,"* He was demonstrating His ability to discern the deepest thoughts of people's heart. In saying, *"I am the life,"* He set an example of practicing whatever he taught (John 14:6).

Jesus spoke the truth, discerned the truth, and practiced the truth all in perfection. He did not need to bring a sin offering, but we do.

Trespass Offering

Lev. 5:14–6:7. Lev. 7:1–10
Restoration and Compensation
The Fourth Offering

The sin offering was a demonstration of man's ignorance defrauding God of what is rightfully His, namely speaking the truth, discerning the truth, and practicing the truth. How clearly and simply Jesus was able to summarize His life and relationship to the Father and declare it to the human race. All sin on earth has its roots in being ignorant in one or more of these three examples.

The kind of animal brought to the altar by the offerer for a sin offering depended on the position he held in society. In the trespass offering, there was only one kind of animal–*a ram without defect*–for all the classes. But now restitution was added, plus a double tithe as a penalty. No hands were laid on its head for identification or substitution. Here was restitution

In the first two offerings it was consecration to God and consecration to man. "Love the Lord your God with all your heart . . . and your neighbor as yourself." In the sin and trespass offerings, we see a similar pair. The sin offering is about my *sin and ignorance toward God in all manner of truth* and the need for a Redeemer to satisfy God's requirements on my behalf. The trespass offering is about *sin and ignorance or indifference toward my fellow man* and the requirement of restitution and the payment of a penalty.

In Ecclesiastes 5:4–6, we have an example of this pair.

"When you make a vow to God, do not be late in paying it, for He takes no delight in fools. Pay what you vow. It is better that you should not vow than that you should vow and not pay. Do not let your speech cause you to sin and do not say in the presence of the messenger of God that it was a mistake. Why should God be angry on account of your voice and destroy the work of your hand?"

Take notice of the tongue toward God and the hand toward man.

Andrew Bonar describes the scene something like this in his book *Leviticus*. The wish of this man to be spoken well of and to appear pious in the eyes of the priest and the people caused him, while attending public worship in the temple, to vow more with his lips than he could or more than he really wished to give. By this rash vow before God, he came under the sin of Lev. 5:1–4. He was not speaking the truth to God, he was not discerning the truth about himself, and not practicing the truth before others. This required a sin offering.

"When the priest came to collect his share of the offering according to the law, the man was tempted to deny that he vowed so much. And so he fell into the sin of trespass mentioned in Lev. 5:15 because he withheld what he promised to the house of God," writes Andrew Bonar in his book *Leviticus*.

So he was to *bring a ram*, the animal of substitution, (as seen in the story of the ram being a substitute offering for Isaac) without defect, chosen from the flock even as Christ was " . . . one that was mighty . . . chosen from the people" (Ps. 89:19). Like the ram.

The priest did *two things* when the ram was brought. He estimated the value of the ram, indicating the value of the offerer's view of the law he had broken, and then added one fifth (a double tithe) because of the attempt to defraud God by withholding a portion for one self.

God's atonement (for sin to be covered) also required *two things*.

There had to be *restoration of what was lost*. God needed to restore all the honor His law lost for a time because of man's failure to keep it.

There had to be *compensation for wrongdoing*. God had to have the honor of His law vindicated by an amount of suffering or penalty.

The active obedience of Jesus provided the first. Every detail of His life expressed how He valued His Father's direction. "I can do nothing on my own. As I hear, I judge" (John 5: 19, 30; 7:16; 8:26, 38; 12:49).

The passive obedience of Jesus provided the second. "My soul is deeply grieved to the point of death" (Matt. 26:38). Jesus passively submitting Himself into the hands of sinful man was to restore the honor of the law by an incomprehensible amount of suffering.

Jesus, in fulfilling the ram as a type, was not estimated very highly by the Sanhedrin at 30 pieces of silver–the price of a slave (Matt. 26:15). Peter held a higher value for the blood of Jesus (I Peter 1:19). Who can tell how high it was valued in the heavenly sanctuary? We know it was high enough to redeem and "put all things in subjection under His feet and gave Him as head over all things to the church" (Eph. 1:22).

We are obligated to what the trespass offering illustrated and what Jesus demonstrated. "Though he is unaware, still he is guilty and shall bear his punishment" (Lev. 5:17). This is not the presumptuous sin of Ps. 19:13 which is to willfully sin. We presume that we can willfully do this thing and not suffer the consequences for it later on.

Paul says "I was formerly a blasphemer and a persecutor and a violent aggressor, and yet I was shown mercy, because I acted ignorantly in unbelief"–I Tim. 1:13.

"So the priest shall make atonement for him concerning his error in which he sinned unintentionally and did not know it, and it shall be forgiven him"–Lev. 5:18.

The blaspheming with his mouth toward God required a sin offering. The violent aggression toward man required a trespass offering. Yet he was shown mercy and was forgiven because faith enabled him to understand and believe that the offerings had been made on his behalf.

By treating ignorance as a sin of such magnitude, God put His people under the solemn duty to inquire into His revealed will. It is not necessary to continue in sin so that grace may abound. *Let the altar do its work* on the sin issues so that we become free to move on toward the holy place.

Defrauding Others

Lev. 6:1–7

Five Examples of Trespassing

Forgiveness and restoration are important to God because without them there is no acknowledging of sin, and His law remains violated. He is equally concerned about the violated rights of man. Paul's own experience of forgiveness enables him to write to the Galatian churches that " . . . even if a man is caught in any trespass, you who are spiritual, restore such a one in a spirit of gentleness, each one looking to yourself, lest you be tempted" (Gal. 6:1).

Failure in trust

Lev. 6:2

This pertains to a person who deceives another in regard to a deposit or a security entrusted to him (Lev. 6:2). You have an estate to manage, anything that is lent to you; a book, or any article.

Paul uses the words of I Tim. 6:20 to convey the meaning. "O, Timothy, guard what has been entrusted to you." Also to the Roman church he writes, "For the gifts and the calling of God are irrevocable" (Rom. 11:29). These have been entrusted to us by God. We are responsible to use them in service and ministry. Any denial of having received them or carelessness in using or keeping them is a trespass in the eyes of God. In doing wrong against your neighbor you have trespassed against God also.

Every commitment or promise we make in life is important. Commitment is an engagement that restricts freedom or action.

I cannot continue to go on seeking my own way and my own pleasure and speaking my own words to God or man. Remember the warning of Ecclesiastes 5:4–6.

Unfairness in partnership or fellowship.
Lev. 6:2

This refers to transactions in public life that are lawful in appearance, but selfish in reality. A present day example would be the expression, "I have my rights," but to have them at another's expense.

In Luke 19:2 there is a man named Zaccheus, chief tax collector. He had a legal position to collect taxes, but had a habit of taking some extra. God's morality was a higher order. As Paul says, "with humility of mind, let each of you regard one another as more important than self" (Phil. 2:3).

It is about others not having to fulfill our responsibilities in life or at work even when we are in position of authority to rule in comfort over them.

Toward government, there needs to be a conscious observance of regulations, commercial laws and taxes.

In II Sam. 24:24, David is purchasing the threshing floor of Araunah, trying to stop the plague he had caused by his census. It is offered to David free of charge, but David says, "I will buy it from you for a price, for I will not offer to the Lord that which has cost me nothing." The census had cost David nothing. Joab was sent out for nine months to do the counting. But 70,000 people died because of David. This had been an act of gross *unfairness in the partnership of David and Israel*; a sad abuse of his position as king.

Taking by Violence.

Lev. 6:2

This is not limited to open assault, beating or robbery. There are strong-willed, determined people who insist on having their own way, exercising authority, irrespective of another's conscience. One can think of wars and death camps, political ideologies, religious ideologies, even the school bully or inner city gangs. These are cases where oppression or hardship or mere power deals with weakness, like Ahab taking Naboth's vineyard (I Kings 22).

Deception—To deceitfully oppress.

Lev. 6:2

A Jew was guilty of this trespass when walking past a neighbor's vineyard and ate more than he would if it had been his own. It can be applied to bribing people to vote, to overloading people with work or overtime, or not paying them as promised (James. 5:4).

The great dragon of Rev. 12:3 has been deceitfully oppressing the people of all nations since the day he lied to Adam and Eve. Think of all the promises made to raise hopes and expectations in people that are then broken. How successful he has been to use one part of the scriptures to destroy another. Jesus gives eight "Woe to you" examples for misusing the scriptures and deceitfully oppressing the people in Matt. 23:13–36, and reminds them of the consequences in verses 37–39.

Keeping things you have found.
Lev. 6:3

We are not to build our joy on the loss of others, thinking they will not miss what they have lost. Every effort must be made to find the owner. Anything Satan has found himself to have control over, he does not relinquish easily. He does go around like a roaring lion seeking whom he can devour (I Pet. 5:8). How easily addictions are formed, and how hard they are to break and be set free of them.

In Exodus 20:5–6, God speaks of Himself as " . . . a jealous God, visiting the iniquities of the fathers upon the children . . . but showing loving kindness to thousands who love Me and keep My commandments." The perverted truths that we are content to live with are the very iniquities God visits upon the third and fourth generation.

God is very jealous to maintain the rights of humanity. His demand for restitution in Ex. 22:1,4, shows He will maintain His violated rights to the very end. The honor of His law will be vindicated. "Fools mock at sin, but among the upright there is good will" (Prov. 14:9).

Andrew Bonar writes the following in his book, *Leviticus*; "Those who do not fear the storm, do not go to the hiding place. Peter loved the risen Savior who relieved him of the load of his denial. The angel of death in Egypt caused Israel to appreciate the blood on the door posts."

If Jesus had not fully satisfied the holy law in *active obedience* and paid the one fifth in His *passive suffering* during His trial and crucifixion, it would have left us without redeeming grace.

The Peace Offering

Lev. 3; Lev. 7:11–38

"Reconciliation"
The Fifth offering

The prophet Amos tells Israel that God was no longer accepting the burnt and grain offering and would no longer have regard for their peace offerings. These three kinds of offerings were called free will offerings because an Israelite was free to bring them.

These three are mentioned first in Leviticus, though the order in which the five offerings were presented was burnt offering, meal offering, sin offering, trespass offering and peace offering.

The sin and trespass offerings were required when guilt became evident to the individual. The priests also brought many other required offerings, including the required public peace offerings at the seven annual feasts and the first days of every month.

It is clear from Amos 5:21–24 and Jeremiah 14:12, that the free will offerings *can be brought in a way God hates*. "I hate, I reject your festivals, . . . Take away from me the noise of your songs. I will not even listen to the sound of your harps."

This happens when the "how to" of religion is taught long after the "why to" has been forgotten.

The altar brings us some understanding of how God illustrated His view of the sin problem, His hatred for it and how His holiness is separated from it. It brings some insight into the holiness of heaven, of living in His presence. We can imagine a little of how the darkness of hell is the compressed horror of all the compiled history of pride, evil, war, suffering, hatred, etc. and the absence of God's ever expanding universe of love, grace, joy, peace, etc.

The *reason* for the altar is sin, and it is at this altar that *Jesus satisfied the needs of God* in regards to holy perfection and *the needs of man* in regards to sin and ignorance. He brought peace between God and man. Friendship is reestablished. Fellowship and praise are now possible.

Therefore the *response* to the altar is a sanctified worship, which can be defined as a relationship of *extreme submission and extravagant love* (Gen. 22:18). Those who know they have free access to God will make abundant use of this and thank Him for it.

This is also what the writer of Hebrews says.

> "Through Him then, let us continually offer up a sacrifice of praise that is the fruit of our lips that give thanks to His name"–Heb. 13:15.

The peace offering illustrates for us *not so much the manner,* but *the effects of atonement and redemption,* such as peace with God, reconciliation, and God conveying blessing upon the offerer or nation.

The peace offering was *shared by all three parties.* The fat was for God, the breast and right shoulder for the priest, and the rest for the offerer. The animal *could be male or female*, a type of deepest friendship.

The laying on of hands was for identifying with the Redeemer as the source of blessing. So it was to be done *at the door of the tabernacle*, demonstrating we have entered into the presence of God, trusting that His grace is sufficient and his promised peace a joyful reward.

The blood was sprinkled around on the altar as a testimony

of the Redeemer's life that brought to us the promised peace and fellowship. This the apostle Paul also writes to the Christian church in Rome.

> "Therefore, having been justified by faith, we have peace with God through our Lord Jesus Christ. Through whom also we have obtained our introduction by faith into this grace where in we stand"–Rom. 5:1,2.

The best portions of the animal offered, namely all *the fat and kidneys and liver*, were placed in the fire of the burnt offering as God's portion. As this best portion came from deep inside the animal, we also need to bring the best of our inward feelings of gratitude of the richest kind.

This was done by Jesus as He poured out His soul "to the point of death" (Mark 14:34), and by "the eternal spirit offered himself . . . to God" (Heb. 9:14), to become "our peace" (Eph. 2:14). His affections toward God and man did not diminish when tested and tried by fire. He was a soothing aroma to God.

In the case of the *male or female sheep*, the portion on the altar is *spoken of as food*, an offering by fire to the Lord (Lev. 3:11), as though God is seated at the table with His people. In Mal. 1:7, the altar is called, "the table of the Lord," which His people treated with contempt.

In this offering, one of three animals could be brought to the tabernacle. In the *bullock/ox,* we see the Lord represented as strong and patient (Lev. 3:1). The *lamb* represents the Lord Jesus as meek and gentle (Lev. 3:6). And in the *goat* we see the Lord as chosen from among us as the one despised and rejected (Lev. 3:12). The goat representing Jesus as taken out of the flock of humanity for the salvation of the rest is like a lion choosing one goat from a flock as its prey to satisfy its hunger, so the death of this one saved the rest of the flock.

Caiaphas said of Jesus, "It is expedient for us that one man should die for the people and that the whole nation should not perish" (John 11:50).

When the offerer could not bring a bull, he brought a sheep or a goat. Jesus was more than just *meek and gentle as a lamb* and increasing in favor. He was also *strong and patient as a bullock* in his service. As *the ram* He was a leader who was hated for His public testimony that their works were evil. And as *the goat* He was *taken from among us* to be our savior, mediator, and peace. God takes great care not to emphasize one part of our Redeemer's work above another.

The Leavened Cake

Lev. 7:11–38

Of the Peace Offering

When the blood had been sprinkled on the altar and the fat burned in the fire, then the breast and right shoulder were separated from the animal and each other. These were known as the heave and wave offerings.

The right shoulder was the heave offering, lifted up to the Lord as ruler of Heaven. It was raised and lowered, then symbolically set aside as a contribution to God, but given by Him to the priests as their due (verse 32). This part was to be boiled or roasted and eaten the same day. Peace with God is to be feasted upon immediately.

The breast was the wave offering moved from side to side for the Lord as ruler of the earth. And it was waved toward and from the altar as a symbol of presenting the offering to God and receiving it back as the priest portion (verse 34). The remaining portion belonged to the offerer and had to be eaten and enjoyed immediately and all consumed within two days or burned.

Peace offerings could be brought for *three reasons*.

One was as an *act of thanksgiving* (Lev. 7:12) for a particular answer to prayer in a time of need. Or it could be for a deliverance from danger on land or storms at sea or for healing from a sickness.

The second was in case of someone *making a vow* (Lev. 7:16). This is well illustrated in the storey of Hannah appealing to God for the particular favor of having a son and vowing to "give him to the Lord all the days of his life" (I Sam. 1:11).

The third was simply *a free will peace offering* (Lev. 7:16) given out of the abundance of the heart for general enjoyment of His blessing. The offerer might see himself expressing his heart's affections to the priest and recognizing him to be the means through which God's blessings came to him. It would remind him of the great high priest who now provides the peace and joy of reconciliation.

Along with these peace offerings was brought a grain offering consisting of *three types of cakes and oil* - the cakes being a type of Christ (and the believer in Christ) and the oil being a type of the Holy Spirit.

There were *"unleavened cakes mixed with oil"* (Lev. 7:12). These would bear witness of the spirit being involved and mixed into the events of our lives to direct and empower.

Then there were *"unleavened wafers spread with oil"* (Lev. 7:12). These would bear witness of the spirit being on our particular callings in life, or to set someone apart for an intended purpose.

And there were *"leavened cakes stirred with oil"* (Lev. 7:13). These leavened cakes bear witness of corruption being still present in my life, but also the Spirit being mixed in to give direction and empowerment.

So in presenting these cakes before God, there was an acknowledgement of His spirit being involved in the general events of ones' life to guide and direct. There was an acknowledgement of the particular callings of our life, and an acknowledgement that there is still corruption present in ones life. Yet because this is a peace offering, the person is reconciled to God.

But *"perfect pardon* does not imply *perfect holiness,"* wrote Andrew Bonar in his book *Leviticus*.

That is why this cake was waved before the Lord as a heave offering (Lev. 7:14). *The offerer holds up before the Lord whatever corruption is still present, to be dealt with as the Lord sees fit.* Psalm

139:23–24 testifies to this. "Search me, O God, and know my heart; try me and know my thoughts; And see if there be any hurtful way in me ..."

I do not hesitate to think that it takes some measure of faith to appreciate everything that God was setting before Israel. But this *faith would awake* a longing for holiness, for fellowship, for wanting to deal with sins instead of living in contentment with it. In contrast, *pride will blind us to our faults*. It won't let us see our iniquities, and it won't let us see the grace of God before us and all around us. Therefore it cannot teach us anything (Titus 2:11–12). Let me illustrate with some history from the Old Testament.

In I Kings 12:20, there begins a story in the year 931 BC. Jeroboam becomes king over the northern ten tribes of Israel, and for the next 200 years, he is remembered as the "one who committed sin, and who made Israel sin" (1 Kings 14:16). Of the 19 kings mentioned who ruled that part of the country after him, 17 have it said of them that "they followed in the way of Jeroboam, and in his sin, which he made Israel to sin." And of those 17, it is said of Ahab, "he did even more."

During the last 50 years of this 200 year period, Amos and Hosea carry on where Elijah and Elisha left off in Israel. Just before Israel's fall and journey into exile in 722 BC, Amos declares God's displeasure with their offerings and sacrifices:

> "I hate, I reject your festivals ... Even though you offer up burnt offerings and your grain offerings, I will not accept them. I will not even look at the peace offerings of your fatlings. Take away from me the noise of your songs ... but let justice roll down like waters and righteousness like an ever- flowing stream"–Amos 5:21–24.

> "Therefore I will make you go into exile beyond Damascus, says the Lord "–Amos 5:27.

Some 100 years later, Jeremiah is prophesying in Jerusalem and carries on where Isaiah and Micah left off. His message to Judah is remarkably the same. " . . . they have healed the brokenness of my people superficially, saying peace, peace, but there is no peace" (Jer. 6:14). " . . . Your burnt offerings are not acceptable, and your sacrifices are not pleasing to me" (Jer. 6:20; 8:11).

The evidence of the temple and altar sacrifices had not changed. Even the prophets were still proclaiming God's warnings and invitations, but it made no difference. How does this happen?

Idolatry is only possible when the inner throne of one's being is not filled with Christ as Lord and King. Then *the leavened cake* is no longer *waved before God as confession of corruption* and the need to be changed.

The Laver

Ex. 30:18–21; 38:8

"Something Round" in Hebrew

As I left the tents of Israel and entered through the gate by faith into the righteousness of God, I would see the great work of redeeming grace before me. I would identify with the substitute on the altar, completely exposed and completely consumed. I would see complete acceptance, complete redemption, complete reconciliation and peace. I would see God's hatred for sin and the judgment of it, and God would see the life represented in the blood and be satisfied.

Having all this imputed to me, I am free to continue the journey toward the holy place where the presence of God dwells.

But I feel like asking the same questions that Micah the prophet asks.

> "With what shall I come to the Lord and bow myself before the God on high? Shall I come to Him with burnt offerings, with yearling calves? Does the Lord take delight in thousands of rams, in ten thousand rivers of oil? Shall I present my first born for my rebellious acts? The fruit of my body for the sin of my soul?"–Micah 6:6–7.

He continues by answering his own questions.

> "He has told you, O man, what is good. And what does the Lord require of you, but to do justice, to love kindness, and to walk humbly with your God"–Micah 6:8.

Now I have the same question Mary had for the angel. "How can this be . . . ?" (Luke 1:34). How shall this justice and love and kindness and humility be born in me? How shall my carnal flesh give birth to what is holy and righteous and kind?

The Redeemer Jesus of the altar has an answer. The Holy Spirit "will take of Me and reveal it to you" (John 16:14). He has a wonderful way of taking what Jesus is and *speaking it into existence* in our own lives. This ongoing work after redemption is called sanctification. The qualities of Jesus' life are imparted to us. It is His perfect holiness, patience, love, Godliness, faith and purity we share in. Jesus is formed in us. All His perfections are made ours entirely. He does not give us the ability to produce by a slow steady process a holiness like His, but it is His holiness in us that becomes visible. Jesus is far more than an example to follow or someone among us. *His life is in us.*

The redemption at the altar is followed by sanctification at the laver. As Jesus says, "He who has bathed needs only to wash his feet, but is completely clean" (John 13:10). The bathing would point to redemption, the washing of the feet to sanctification.

Paul uses a different illustration to point this out to the Ephesians. " . . . Christ also loved the church and gave himself for her that He might sanctify and cleanse her with the washing of water by the word" (Eph. 5:25–26 NKJV). First He gave Himself. That is our redemption, which gives us our *position in Christ.* Then He washed her with water, by the word. That is sanctification, which tells us that our *condition requires it.*

We are assured that "He who began a good work in you will perfect it until the day of Christ Jesus" (Phil. 1:6). And so there is a need to "Work out your salvation in fear and trembling"(Phil. 2:12).

If we are to draw near to God in the holy place and handle the holy things of God, then it is the Word of God that must do the work.

John begins his gospel by saying, "In the beginning was the Word, and the Word was with God, and the Word was God. He was in the beginning with God" (John 1:1–2). "And the Word became flesh and dwelt among us" (John 1:14). This Word came not only to redeem at the altar, but also to sanctify at the laver. Where the altar used blood for cleansing, the laver uses water *a type of Jesus that washes with the Word.*

In Rom. 12:2, we read, "not to be conformed to this world, but be 'transformed' by the renewing of your minds." The same word is used of Jesus when "He was transfigured before them" on the mountain (Matt. 17:2). It means "metamorphose"–to change from a caterpillar to butterfly. The influence of the Word of God must have that effect upon our mind.

Imagine having all the carnal influences of culture and media upon our minds and hearts overruled by the Word and Spirit of God. This was seen in the face of Stephen as he was before the council (Acts 6:15). In chapter 7:55, we can read that his transformed mind was given to see "the glory of God and Jesus at the right hand of God; and he said Behold, I see the heavens opened up and the Son of Man standing at the right hand of God."

To us also is promised that " . . . we all with unveiled face beholding as in a mirror the glory of the Lord, are being *transformed* (same word in Greek as *transfigured*) into the same image from glory to glory . . ." (II Cor. 3:18).

There are *no dimensions given* for the Laver because the Word of God is without dimension or limit in its effect. It is described only as a *round basin with a base.* In Hebrew, the word for laver means "something round."

Both the basin and the base were made of *the polished bronze looking glasses* of the women who served at the door of the tabernacle (Ex. 38:8).

These ladies willingly offered up the means to enhance their own personal appearance in order to provide for the priest-hood a means of cleansing from acquired pollution. Without this washing, there was no access permitted into the holy place and presence of God, on penalty of death.

The laver would not be a place for *admiration* of self, but a place for *inspection* of self. It was *to reveal the priest to himself* as God would see him in His presence. Therefore the laver speaks of surrender—a willingness to part with what was calculated to make something of self.

Functions of the Laver

Ex. 30:19–21

Reveal Wash Instruct

"How can a young man cleanse his way? By taking heed according to your word.......Your word have I hidden in my heart, that I might not sin against You"–Ps. 119:9,11 (NKJV).

"Now you are clean through the Word I have spoken unto you"–John 15:3.

This Word now functions as our laver.

When we determine to go beyond the bronze altar and take part in the ministries of the table of bread and lampstand and Altar of Incense, then we must learn to use the laver.

"Who may ascend into the hill of the Lord? Or who may stand in His holy place? He who has clean hands and a pure heart."–Ps. 24:3,4.

In the laver, we will see not only a reflection of ourselves in its message; it also brings a dependence on the Spirit (John 16:14), a commitment to obedience (John 14:15), a conviction of the truth (John 17:17–19), a discipline to our choices (Phil. 4:8), and God-centered desires (James 4:5).

The same Laver that reveals defilement also has the means to cleanse. But it *is not just imputed to me* like the redemption at the altar. Nothing can be added to that finished work. The laver *requires participation*. The priest had to take water *from* the laver and wash his hands and feet. We are not to pollute the water of the Word by exaggerated emphasis on a preferred text.

The laver is a type of Jesus the Word. Cleansing by this Word is not automatic. The Word of God is to us what soap and water is to dirt. The clothes don't know how the soap and water work, but when they flow through the clothes, all the dirt comes out. All of God's Word has cleansing properties, but it must be read to have it flow through our minds.

The church will not be cleansed by exorcism, healings, tongues, ecumenism, music, etc., but by the Word. The Word proclaimed may very well result in these things happening, but it is the Word, not what it produces, that cleanses people.

We need to "draw near (the presence of God in the holy place) with a sincere heart in full assurance of faith, having our hearts sprinkled clean from an evil conscience and our bodies washed with pure water" (Heb. 10:22).

They shall wash their hands and their feet "*that they may not die*" (Ex. 30:19–21). That is a severe penalty.

Paul understood its severity when he warned the Corinthian church about "eating and drinking in an unworthy manner" (I Cor. 11:27). "For this reason, many among you are weak and sick and some have died" (I Cor. 11:30).

The priest was to wash before going into God's presence and before going to the altar. These are two different things.

In the holy place, we don't work in His presence, and at the Altar, we don't worship people. *In His presence*, we receive instructions. *Leaving His presence*, we carry them out.

In His presence, we are as Mary sitting at His feet (Luke 10:39), listening to Him. Leaving His presence, we are as Martha, doing His bidding (verse 40).

We need to learn what to love and what to hate as Jesus did.

Saul lost his kingdom for not hating what God hated. Israel lost their land for not loving what God loved (His Word).

We need to learn again that the holy place, the naos, (the sanctuary), was meant to be the place where *we come to be impressed* by God, while evangelism was *going out of His presence to express* these impressions to a world that does not know Him.

My observation is that today, we go into the world to be impressed by it, and then come into His presence, to express ourselves as our means of evangelism, as if God needs to be evangelized.

The altar and laver have different purposes.

The altar gives me *my position in Christ*; it is secure. My Redeemer Jesus has the power to keep me safe. But it is like the leavened wafer said, "perfect pardon does not mean perfect holiness."

The laver reveals *my condition in Christ.* It is imperfect and has the leaven of sin still in it. It needs to be worked on and cleaned up. We need to memorize and apply the Word to our problems so we have answers when tempted. So Jesus can say, "Now you are clean through the word I have spoken" (John 15:3).

The altar and laver had brass exteriors, and both were in the outer court and were symbols of cleansing. The altar of *wood, overlaid with bronze,* illustrated the humanity of Jesus that was overlaid with the judgment of man's sin. The laver was *solid bronze,* illustrating God's Word to be *without the wood of human thought.*

" . . . the word I spoke is what will judge him at the last day" (John 12:48–50). It was, is and will be the final word of authority.

The altar	The laver
~ was for every one who came	~was for the priest only
~was for fire	~was for water
~was for the rebellious heart	~for the contaminated walk
~uses blood for cleansing	~uses water for cleansing
~deals with depravity	~deals with defilement
~cleans past, inherited sin	~cleans present, acquired sin
~offers provisional cleansing (God's law is satisfied)	~offers practical cleansing (man's defilement is removed)

Jesus Our Laver

Matt. 9:4

He Knows What Is In Man

The washing at the laver is declared a statute forever (Ex. 30:21). Israel is also declared to be a nation before God forever (Jer. 31:36). Since Israel is still among us as a nation among nations, then this washing at the laver must also still be in effect.

The Word of God is still a source of instruction (II Tim. 3:16). It is still a discerner of the heart (Heb. 4:12). Faith still comes by hearing the Word of God (Rom. 10:17). It still has *creative power* like when He said, "Let there be," and "there was" (Gen. 1:3). Jesus said, "If you abide in me and my words abide in you, ask whatever you wish and it shall be done for you" (John 15:7). That can be understood to imply, if it's not around, it shall be made for you (or spoken into existence).

At the feast of Passover:

> "many believed in His name, beholding His signs which He was doing.(and speaking into existence) But Jesus on His part was not entrusting Himself to them for He knew all men, and because He did not need anyone to bear witness concerning man, for He Himself knew what was in man."– John 2:23–25.

Many believed in and followed Him, while He had no faith in them. He knew why most of them followed Him.

There is a faith to which Jesus makes no response and to

which He is strangely silent. Because *He knew what was in them*. This quality of discernment characterized the life of Jesus. He draws people and then divides them (Luke 12:51).

No man can long be insincere in the presence of Christ. Jesus pierces every disguise. Throughout His life, He demonstrated the ability *to speak, discern and practice the truth*, but many were not willing to be sanctified by it. In the presence of Christ, no man misquotes himself. The deepest depth of people's hearts becomes expressed. "For out of the abundance of the heart, the mouth speaks" (Matt. 12:34 NKJV).

This discerning power of Jesus is important to notice because it inspires obedience and directs us to look for guidance in the realm of faith. This faith is not only the beginning of a new life, but also the sustaining power that allows Jesus to get at the very roots of my life.

Positive thinking can never deal with the issue of sin, so it is important not to submit to any man's philosophy; it is entirely inadequate.

Draw near to Jesus, who knows everything about what is in the human heart. He knows our heredity, our handicaps, the powers of our circumstances, *and knowing everything*, He makes allowance for everything as no one else does.

The love of Jesus is not based on ignorance as with us. We much prefer that others remain ignorant of at least some part of our life. But with Jesus, it is based on the *fullest knowledge*. He knows what is in man, even of all our days before we come to Him for salvation; all the hindrances to our faith and distrust of which we are afraid to speak. Things like rejection, humiliation, suffering, pain and death.

He knows better than we, "that while we were yet sinners, Christ died for us" (Rom. 5:8). He estimates everything at its fullest moral or spiritual value. He knows us completely and deals with us, not according to what we think is fair or right, but according to His own infinite grace as He put it on display at the altar of sacrifice.

In the encounter with the helpless paralytic, Jesus said, "Your sins are forgiven" (Matt. 9:2). The leaders who heard this thought it was blasphemy. To them "Jesus *knowing their thoughts* said, 'Why are you thinking evil in your hearts?" (verse 4).

In Matt. 22:18, Jesus is asked about giving to Caesar. He *perceived their wickedness* and said, "Why are you testing me, you hypocrites?"

And then can you imagine the surprise in Matt. 7:21 that these people had? They had a very successful ministry, prophesying and casting out demons and saying Lord, Lord, and performing many miracles. It must have come as a shock for them to hear Jesus say, *"You workers of iniquity."* (or lawlessness). But then, you cannot measure truth by success.

What then does the faith look like that Jesus does respond to and knows to be in man?

It is faith *drawn* by a hunger and thirst for God and truth (Matt. 5:6).

It is a faith that *recognizes* the contrast between the holy standard of God and our condition. The carnality of "The heart is deceitful and desperately wicked. Who can know it" (Jer. 17:9)?

It is a faith that *brings conviction* of sin and expresses sorrow for sin, not merely sin's consequences. Paul could say, "Oh, wretched man that I am. Who will deliver me from this body of death" (Rom. 7:24)?

Faith brings a *realization* of our emptiness, weakness, need and insufficiency. He provides for these according to His riches (Eph. 3:16).

Faith compels a *surrender* to Christ, who can supply all the sin-created needs of our life.

"That you may know, what is the hope of His calling, what are the riches of the glory of His inheritance in the saints and what is the surpassing greatness of His power toward us who believe?"–Eph. 1:18–19.

It is a faith that *believes.*

"In returning [to me] and resting [in Me], you shall be saved. In quietness and [trusting] confidence shall be your strength"–Isa. 30:15 AMP.

Jesus responds to faith that *works by love*; faith that *is responsive to His call* in an ever increasing comprehension of His will.

Who Comes to the Laver?

II Kings 22

People Who Need Jesus

After reading the last chapter, we might ask what kind of people are these that come to the laver. There are plenty of examples. I'll mention a few.

Josiah was eight years old when he became king of Judah. His father and grandfather had desecrated the temple. After growing up for another eight years, he initiated a clean up in the temple.

The high priest finds a book of the law and reads it to King Josiah. He tears his clothes and finds out from the prophetess Huldah what the consequences are going to be for Judah. The news is not good for Judah. But to Josiah she says, "because your heart was tender and *you humbled yourself* before the Lord . . . you have torn your clothes and wept before Me, I truly have heard you, declares the Lord" (II Kings 22:19).

One needs to read the next chapter, II Kings 23, to get an idea of how much of the idolatry of the nations had come even into the temple itself. Like in verse 4; "to bring out of the temple all the vessels that were made for Baal, for Asher and for all the hosts of heaven." And verse 10, where he destroyed the altar of Molech, so that no more children would be burned alive as offerings to this god.

People could go from this altar to the one in the temple, a short distance to the north, and there present other offerings to a variety of gods.

The clean up of the temple that led to the discovery of the law would indicate that what had been passed on by word of mouth had been very selective (II Kings 22:11).

It is so *convenient to forget what we don't like*. Perhaps the laver had not been used for a long time either. This was a time when Judah could worship any god anywhere, anytime, and Israel was already taken into exile 80 years before for doing the same things.

For Josiah at 16 years of age, it was quite an undertaking to take on all the pagan priests and prophets. His humility is rewarded by God.

> "And before him (some 400 years) there was no king like him who turned to the Lord with all his heart and with all his soul and with all his might according to the law of Moses: nor did any arise like him after him"–II Kings 23:25.

In Gen. 32, we find Jacob on his way back from Laban after 21 years. He is wrestling with an angel. Hosea 12:4 says "Jacob wrestled with the angel and prevailed. He wept and sought His favor." For 21 years the promise of God in Gen 28:10–15 had not been realized.

Though he is certain the promise was from God (Gen. 28:17), He is not certain God will keep it (verse 20).

Though this event may have occurred almost 500 years before there was a laver, Jacob's wrestling is still a beautiful picture of someone *who wrestles with God over His promised word*. He has a promise. He needs God to fulfill it, so he wrestles all night and prevails and says, "I will not let you go until you bless me" (Gen. 32:26).

Jacob had a need, and *God loves the one who needs Him*. He leaves with a new name and new song. "I have seen God face to face, yet my life has been preserved" (Gen. 32:30).

Jesus spoke His transforming power into the sin-created needs of: people with *unstable resolve* but fervent love, like the father who cried out on behalf of his son, "I do believe; help my unbelief" (Mark 9:24); people with *stained reputation*, but earnest devotion, like the Samaritan woman who testified to her city in which many came to believe saying, "Come and see a man who told me all the things that I have done" (John 4:29); people of *secular work but simple trust*, like the centurion who said on behalf of his paralyzed servant suffering in great pain, " . . . just say the word and my servant will be healed" (Matt. 8:8); people who were *slow of understanding, but became men of dauntless courage*, like the disciples who, after the feast of Pentecost, "began to speak the word of God with great boldness."

On many previous occasions Jesus had used the circumstances of events in the lives of these disciples to bring growth to their meager faith. Four times He had addressed their "little faith."

He taught them not to worry by having a troubled or uneasy mind. "O men of little faith . . . do not be anxious then, saying, 'what shall we eat?' or 'What shall we drink?' or 'With what shall we clothe ourselves'" (Matt. 6:30–31)?

He taught them not to fear or be afraid of an emotion caused by impending evil such as wind and wave and sea. "Why are you timid, you men of little faith" (Matt. 8:26)?

He taught them not to trust the feeling of doubt but to trust and stand on His word, even when walking on water. "Oh you of little faith, why did you doubt" (Matt. 14:31)?

He taught them to remember all the way that He had led them, and not to try to reach conclusions by connecting the reasoning thoughts of their minds. "You men of little faith, why do you discuss among yourselves that you have no bread" (Matt 16:8)?

Then there were people like Mary, Martha, and Lazarus who were of *meager attainment and means but of grateful loyalty*. (John 11); And there were the people who *were poor, brokenhearted and maimed*, but who had a passion for His holiness (Luke 14:13,21).

It is into the lives of people like these that Jesus, the Laver, speaks the transforming power of His Word. It is to these that Jesus commits Himself.

"And when they had prayed, the place where they had gathered was shaken and they were all filled with the Holy Spirit and began to speak the Word of God with boldness"– Acts 4:31.

The Laver as Councilor

Col. 3:16

The Word of Christ and The Word About Christ

The gate is that point of choosing between leaving the wisdom of the world and by faith stepping into the foolishness of God.

The altar is that place where we understand that the foolishness of God's redemption is far wiser than the wisdom of man's pride.

Now at the laver we meet the councilor, Jesus, *who is the Word that became flesh*, who guides, corrects, exhorts, and teaches us to sanctify and set ourselves apart for His intended purpose.

For this to be realized, it would do us well to receive the Word as our operator and service manual. Its instructions ought to be read and followed. That's why Paul exhorts the Colossians to "let the word of Christ dwell in you richly." He is the designer of life and author of the manual. As Jesus said, *"the word I spoke* is what will judge him at the last day" (John 12:48).

In Exodus 25:9 God says to Moses:

> "According to all that I am going to show you as the pattern of the tabernacle and the pattern of all its furniture, just so you shall construct it."

So "Bezalel and Oholiab and every skilful person in whom the Lord had put skill and understanding" (Ex. 36:1) were not free to make this an artistic expression of their own imagination.

Some 500 years later, David has the same message for Solomon. *"All this the Lord made me understand* in writing by His hand upon me, all the details of this pattern" (I Chron. 28:11–19). The sad record of Old Testament disobedience spoken of and warned against by the prophets for centuries carries on into the New.

Jesus warned that "In vain do they worship Me, teaching as doctrines, the precepts of men" (Matt. 15:9). "And why do you yourselves transgress the commandment of God for the sake of your tradition" (Matt 15:3)?

For eight different reasons He addresses the scribes and Pharisees by saying "Woe to you hypocrites" (Matt. 23:13–29). "You worship that which you do not know" (John 4:22).

In the last sentence recorded by Matthew, Jesus once again emphasizes a need to "teach them to *observe all that I command you*" (Matt. 28:20).

Paul, in keeping with this instruction, writes to the Roman church and warns about

> "men who suppress the truth in unrighteousness, … For even though they knew God, they did not honor Him as God, or give thanks, but they became futile in their speculations and their foolish heart was darkened. Professing to be wise, they became fools and exchanged the glory of the incorruptible God for an image in the form of corruptible man–Rom. 1:18–21.

> "So beware, see that no one takes you captive through philosophy and empty deception, according to the traditions of men, according to the elementary principles of the world rather than according to Christ"–Col. 2:8.

As God said to Moses, "Whatever I command you, you shall

be careful to do. You shall not add to it or take away from it" (Deut. 12:32).

Knowing how important this was prompted Jesus to say, "Do not think that I came to abolish the law or the prophets, . . . but to fulfill" (Matt. 5:17).

Why was God so adamant about this principle?

So that Israel would not do like the nations God would drive out before them. These would sacrifice their own children in the fires of their altars as an expression of their devotion to their gods.

Did their gods ask too much?

No. God asked the same of Abraham. It was only when God stopped Abraham that he understood offering Isaac would not have been enough. Man can never *offer too much or enough* for the sin of his soul. Abraham had said to Isaac, "God will provide for Himself the lamb for the burnt offering" (Gen. 22:8). And God did; " . . . and behold, behind him a ram caught in a thicket" (verse 13).

Why do people want to worship God as Israel and the gentiles did? Why not offer to God a life "transformed by the renewing of the mind" and "let the word of God dwell in you richly?"

A long period of church history prior to the reformation had a practice of thinking, "Whatever the Word of God *does not expressly forbid,* that we can do." That produced what is called the "Age of Darkness." This thinking is again becoming popular.

The reformation restored the practice of only what *God has expressly commanded*, that we must obey. That makes for a big problem if we don't know what God said.

When Paul uses the phrase *"word of Christ,"* it refers to that which has Christ as its author; for example, "all scripture is inspired by God" (II Tim. 3:16). But it also refers to that which *is about Christ*; for example, " . . . all things that are written about me in the law of Moses" (Luke 24:44).

An example of Jesus applying this distinction is in (John 5:38–39):

> "You do not have His word abiding in you, (the word about Christ) for you do not believe Him who He sent" (the word of Christ who is speaking to you).

> "You search the scriptures because you think that in them (the word about Christ) you have eternal life, and it is these that bear witness of me." (the word of Christ who is speaking to you).

So in the laver (the scriptures) we find the Word of Christ and the word about Christ. These are now to *"dwell in you richly."* (Col. 3:16). So we will have the mind of Christ to council one another.

Our Union With Christ

Rom. 6:11

A Work In Progress

The word of Christ and about Christ produces in us not only the mind of Christ but also our union with Christ. In Rom. 6:1–11, Paul writes,

> "Don't you know that all of us who have been baptized into Christ have also been baptized into His death? . . . as Christ was raised from the dead through the glory of the Father, so we too might walk in newness of life . . . now if we have died with Christ, we believe that we shall also live with Him . . . Even so, consider yourself dead to sin (our union with sin is dead), but alive to God in Christ Jesus" (our union with Christ is made to live).

In Psalm 69, David is lamenting his circumstances. Next to Psalm 22, it is the most quoted Psalm in the New Testament. Where Psalm 22 deals with the death of Christ, Psalm 69 deals with the life of Christ. This is the Psalm of His humiliation and rejection. Verses 4, 8, 9, 21, and 25 are all quoted in the New Testament and applied to Jesus, yet true of David's experience.

Now look at verse 5 in the New King James Version.

> "Oh God, You know my foolishness and my sins are not hidden from You."

This was certainly true of David. But can this confession of David also be applied to Jesus? If II Cor. 5:21 is true, then it can. For Jesus was made sin for us. Our sin was imputed to Him, and His righteousness to us. So there are parts of the Psalms that you cannot apply to Christ unless you *see Him in union with His people*.

There are also parts of the Psalms you cannot apply to yourself unless you *see yourself in union with Christ*. For example: Ps. 18:16–24:

> "The Lord has rewarded me according to my righteousness, according to the cleanness of my hands. For I have kept the way of the Lord, I was also blameless with Him."

These statements are certainly true of Jesus, but not of David unless the righteousness of Jesus had been imputed to David.

In this union with Christ, I can sing this Psalm as true for me, and Jesus could sing them as true for Him. To sing the Psalms is to sing with Christ Himself, the truth of this *great mystery of Christ in union with His people*.

This union of Christ brought us other benefits as well.

A new commandment

In Christ the law was realized for the first time. He was "the end for looking to the law for righteousness" (Rom. 10:4). Look to Jesus to see what it means to love the Lord your God with all your heart, soul, mind and strength, and your neighbor as yourself. In 1 John 2:7, the apostle says first that he is *"not writing a new commandment"* but an old one they "have had from the beginning," which is "the word you have heard." Then he goes on to say, *"I am writing a new commandment to you, which is true in Him"* (I John 2:8). Meaning it is realized in Jesus. Whoever keeps His word, in him the love of God has truly been perfected (verse 5). The old commandments were written on tablets of stone. This new commandment is now written upon the hearts of all believers and will be on the hearts of all Israel.

> "I will put My law within them ... they shall all know Me, from the least of them to the greatest of them," or " ... Israel also shall cease from being a nation before Me forever."–Jer. 31:33–36

It is the same law but placed in a new container.

A new covenant

God had an everlasting covenant with Abraham and Israel as a nation (Jer. 31:36). And yet in verse 31 God declares "the days are coming when I will make a new covenant with the house of Israel and Judah." This would be a circumcision of the heart (Rom. 2:29), by the Spirit of God (John 3:3–6) producing the birth of the born again believer. The covenant promise is the same everlasting one. It is the embodiment that is new. The outward evidence has changed from circumcision of the flesh to cups of communion. "This cup which is poured out for you is the new covenant in My blood" (Luke 22:20).

A new creation

"If any man be in Christ, he is a new creation" (II Cor. 5:17). We are not yet born into new bodies. Yet God takes the old bodies and begins to form a new man by working His mercy and grace in the human heart to conform it to the image of Christ until the day of resurrection and completion (Rom. 8:29–30).

A new song

When David says to sing *a new song*, he is not saying throw away the old ones. In Psalm 40:2, David had just come out of a pit of miry clay, which may have been his adultery and murder. It's possible his confession in Psalm 51 put him back on the rock of forgiveness, mercy and grace. It was God who *"put a new song in my mouth"* and led him to prophesy; "I delight to do Your will O my God and Your law is within my heart" (Ps. 40:8 NKJV).

This phrase "new song" is used six times in the Psalms, (33, 40, 96, 98, 144, 149) and is used in the context of Christ's salvation and ruling authority. It has nothing to do with pleasing carnal flesh or the latest compact disc.

When Paul writes in Col. 3:16 "to teach and admonish one another with *psalms, hymns and spiritual songs,*" he is not suggesting that songs are spiritual and the other two are not. In Eph. 6:12, he writes about our struggle being "against the *rulers,* the *powers* and *world forces* of darkness." He is saying *all three are of the darkness.* In II Thess. 2:9, where he writes of the lawless one coming "with all *power, signs,* and false *wonders,*" he is saying *all three are false.* Think of the miracles, signs, and wonders of Jesus. All three were done by Jesus. Or the commandments, statutes and judgments of the Lord. One is not more true than the other.

Acts chapters 6 and 7, record the story of Stephen, full of *grace, power* and *wonders.* One is not more important than another. He is brought before a contentious Council not born again nor speaking the language of Spirit and truth. He uses a lengthy history lesson to *introduce his audience to his new song* starting in verse 51.

He was not applauded as he gazed into heaven and spoke *his new song* of seeing "the heavens opened and the Son of Man standing at the right hand of God." Instead, he was stoned to death for not withholding a part of the whole gospel. Stephen was *in union with Christ* in his *life, testimony, new song and death.* One part of his life was not more important then another.

Atonement Money

Ex. 30:11–16

To Acknowledge Ownership

As we leave the laver and approach the tent of the tabernacle, we notice a lot of silver under the boards. Approximately five tons.

Exodus is a book about redemption. In Egypt, Israel was a people in slavery needing to be redeemed, and according to God's promise to Abraham, this redemption begins to take place when Moses is sent back to Egypt. The *purchase of the redeemed* was by the payment of a ransom. In this case, the means of redemption is seen in the blood of a lamb put on the doorpost of people's houses and God saying, "When I see the blood, I will pass over" (Ex12:13). The blood was used as an illustration of the Redeemer's own life. When God sees this applied to our own life, His judgment passes over.

In the unfolding story of Israel's journey, we see the might and power of the Redeemer Himself as He led them through the Sea. They were buried with Him in death and on to the other side, being raised with Him into a new life. There we see *the privilege of the redeemed* worshipping God, singing the song of Moses. "You in Your mercy have led forth the people whom You have redeemed." At Mount Horeb (Ex.33:6), we see *the duty of the redeemed* as being obedient to God, as He spoke to them the terms of this covenant of redemption and ratified it with sacrifice and sprinkling of blood. It was concluded with a covenant meal on the mountain, celebrating this new relationship (Ex. 24:11).

So far, everything was provided by God for Israel. Now, in Ex. 30:11, God requires *a response from His redeemed*. Israel was not redeemed, so they could do their own thing. It was now Israel's turn to pay a ransom. Why a second ransom? Was there something missing in the first? No, this ransom was connected with the numbering of Israel.

In the book of Numbers, this is all spelled out. (See chapter on Assigning Responsibility). This numbering designated ownership of the people. A farmer counts his own sheep because he owns them.

God, having redeemed His people, *had ownership* over them and therefore the right to designate how they would serve Him.

In Dan. 5:26, God pronounces to Belshazzar that, "He has numbered your kingdom and put it to an end." In Dan. 4:25, God has a message for Nebuchadnezzar. "Seven periods of time will pass over you until you recognize that the Most High is ruler over the realm of mankind and bestows it on whomever He wishes." God guards this right.

So when David numbers Israel, I Chron. 21:1–4, he was stepping on what was rightfully God's alone; the ownership of Israel.

God as Redeemer of Israel had the right to not only count, but in so doing, to designate where each part would camp, the order of travel, the exact details of the tabernacle, who would serve where, and every other detail.

In Exodus 12, *Israel is redeemed by blood*. In Ex. 30, *Israel acknowledges His ownership* of them as His numbered people. This money is called an offering to the Lord.

Every Israelite over 20 was to give a ransom for himself of ½ a shekel, or *10 gerahs*. It was like Israel paying its first tithe and giving a portion of everything received from God back to Him. Ten is the number of responsibility, and here they were learning it by personal experience.

So Israel *is not buying* its redemption. That was already secured. They are *acknowledging their responsibility* as one who is owned.

Less than 10 gerahs is not enough any more than keeping nine commandments was enough. The Law was fully realized in the Redeemer's own life. Jesus paid the 10 gerahs in full on man's behalf.

It was according to the Shekel of the Sanctuary, meaning that Jesus was measured by God's standard.

The required ransom was the same for rich and poor because redemption was not according to one's ability, position, riches, or poverty. The great prophet and apostle stand in need of the same atonement, covered by the same blood as the poorest Israelite.

This atonement money *provided the foundation* for the tabernacle boards and pillars (Ex. 38:24–31). Here was the resting place for the presence of God dwelling in the middle of His people.

His presence was based on their redemption, and the redeemed providing a place for Him.

In the outer court, *people needed to look up* to notice the silver caps and rails that testified of their need for atonement. Inside the tabernacle, *God's dwelling place and presence rested on* silver sockets, testifying of His satisfaction with this atonement.

"It was a memorial of the children of Israel before the Lord. It was a lasting testimony before God that a ransom was paid. People might barely comprehend it, but the memorial was there. Even as we now may barely comprehend our redemption in the memorial of the Lord's table." writes A.W. Pink in his book *Gleanings in Exodus.*

As Israel was required to acknowledge the responsibility of now being the people of God, so also our lives should present the evidence that we are not our own but belong to our faithful redeemer Jesus Christ.

God is not a benevolent dictator. He abides in us by invitation, so I must provide a place for Him. I must pay the ransom of making my heart the place of His throne.

The Gold Covered Boards

Ex. 26:15

To Provide A Dwelling Place

The silver sockets of one talent or about 100 pounds each, provided a foundation for boards to be set on. This amounted to over 5 tons of silver for the foundation. These boards were the framework. Each board was 1½ cubits (about 75cm) wide, and 10 cubits (about 5m) high. Each *side had 20 boards* side by side. The *rear had 6 boards* plus *two corner* boards. Each board was held in place at the bottom by *two tennons* ("Hands" in Hebrew) that fitted into two silver sockets (Ex.38:27).

Along the outside of the boards were *three rows of rings* attached to each board. Through these rings went *wooden poles* to tie all the boards together. The middle pole went the entire length of each of the three sides. The top and bottom row were in two pieces.

The *front had five columns or pillars* from which the door or curtain was hung. Each of these items was made of the same acacia wood, which was translated into Greek as "incorruptible wood."

It describes the untainted and incorruptible manhood of Jesus. "He knew no sin" (I Cor. 5:21). And Mark 1:24 writes of Him as, "The Holy one of God."

None of this wood was visible, for it was *overlaid with gold*. No matter how beautiful this polished wood may have been, it needed to be covered. In the presence of God, only the divinity of Jesus was seen. Gold was a type of the Deity of Jesus, representing the perfections of God.

There is nothing that alters gold. It is not affected by air, fire will not burn it, acid does not destroy it, being buried does not deteriorate it, it may be melted and remelted without oxidation and can be beaten so thin that one grain covers 56 sq. in.(350sq. cm.) at 1/282,000"(1/11,280mm) thin. One ounce can cover a silver wire 1600 km. long, and can be drawn into a wire 150 meters. long.

The boards were *placed standing up*, even as Christ was upright in all His ways. Mankind is the fallen race. They were *side by side*, as each act of Jesus ministry followed the one before. They were equal in their *height of 10 cubits*. Ten speaks of human responsibility, and we as the human race were charged with accountability to God. Jesus, who as the Son of God became Man, glorified His Father on earth in the place of human accountability. He never kept one of the 10 commandments more perfectly than another.

The *1½ cubit width* tells us that Jesus was more than man. He magnified the image in which man was created, and He more than kept the law.

The *two corner boards* gave stability to the whole structure. Corner stones are twice mentioned by the prophets. "Behold I lay in Zion. . . . a precious corner stone." (Isa. 28:16). "The stone which the builders rejected has become the chief corner stone" (Ps 118:22).

These boards made a place of *habitation* for the presence of God and the *ministry* of the priesthood. They *surrounded* the furniture that speaks of the provisions that God brought to man in Jesus. They made a place to *display* the curtains above and for the door to *enter* and the veil to *keep out*.

On these boards were *carried* the weight of the curtains and coverings that speak of the glories of the Father's House and the weight of divine government spoken of by Isaiah 22:20–25.

Eliakim means *God will establish*. What was prophesied of him also foreshadowed what would be true of the coming Messiah. "I will entrust him with authority" (verse 21). " . . . I will set the key of the house of David on his shoulder. When he opens, no one will shut. When he shuts, no one will open" (verse 22). And " . . . he will become a throne of glory to his father's house" (verse 23).

The responsibilities of the *weight of the divine government* always pressed on Him. There was His work as the Son of God, as sinless man, as substitution for man. He was to live His life as servant, as king, as leader of His people, as obedient, submissive and humble. These were all part of the fullness of God that dwelt in Him and was carried by Him. Of all this fullness the church is presently to partake and ministers to others.

The boards were 48 in number, which is 6 times 8, or 4 times 12. Four is the number for earth, six the number of man, eight the number of new beginning, and twelve of governmental perfection.

Putting the meanings together, there is a picture of Jesus bringing *new life and government* to man on the earth.

The *two hands* at the bottom of the boards may well speak of the prophets and apostles joining themselves to the great work of the Redeemer. (Eph. 2:20). Through these hands flowed the treasures of His father's kingdom into the redeemed on earth.

The *five bars* on each of the three sides were for tying the boards together, and give structural unity and strength.

These may well have pointed to the function of the leadership of Israel as they reigned and ruled with Him. The *priests and Levites* were represented by the lower set, then the ministry of *prophet* in the middle, and then *kings and elders* represented by the upper set of bars.

The New Testament parallel would be *Apostles and prophets*

for the lower set of two bars, since they are foundational (Eph. 2:20); then *evangelist* for the center bar, since through them the evangel or gospel of good news was to go into the whole world (Eph. 4:11); and *pastors and teachers* would be represented by the upper set of bars. They shepherd the flock and instruct to keep the unity of the church, implying that today the members of Christ's church are the boards standing side by side as the habitation of God's presence.

The Door

Ex. 26:36

From Judgment to Glory

Eight days after the birth of John the Baptist, Zacharias regains his speech and makes a remarkable prophecy, saying in part that John's purpose was to prepare His ways.

> "To give to His people the knowledge of salvation by the forgiveness of their sins, because of the tender mercy of our God, with which the Sunrise from on high shall visit us, to shine upon those who sit in darkness and the shadow of death, to guide our feet into the way of peace."–Luke 1:77–79.

After the fateful event of eating from the forbidden tree, cherubim guarded the east entrance to the tree of life. Mankind was driven from the place where God had communicated with him. Because of sin, *man now walked in the place of darkness*, fear and death. Being outside of the revealing light of God's presence, he has both loved it and feared it.

From then on, animal offerings reminded him of his need for substitution, pointing to the historical the day Zacharias speaks of and to which Simeon adds,

> "For my eyes have seen Thy salvation . . . A light of revelation to the Gentiles."–Luke 2:32).

To Moses, a great deal more is revealed of this coming Redeemer in the construction of the tabernacle. It also had an entrance facing east like the Garden of Eden, but this entrance was not marked by Cherubim. Here was an *entrance that was attractive*. It was meant to draw people and invite them in to enjoy the grace provided.

Here was the fullness of the Redeemer in type, illustrating in detail everything He would do to restore the broken relationship between God and man. He, *the light of the world, would shine into the darkness* of man's ignorance and reveal the way back into the presence of God's peace.

Man was never meant to be only an observer to all of God's provisions at the altar. He was meant to be a partaker of all the privileges and responsibilities. The washing at the laver provided council and instruction in preparation for entrance through the next door.

This door was 10 by 10 cubits or about 5 by 5 meters; *twice as high* as the gate but only *½ as wide*. Sin's dominion over us is terminated at the altar. Our view on holiness is narrowed, and our view of God's purity and perfections is heightened by the laver. Though the area of the two entrances is the same, our focus is redirected *from the carnal beside us* to the *glorious perfections above us.*

This door is *woven* of the same fine twisted white linen and colors as the first gate. The same Hebrew word is also used of the infant *woven and wrought* in its mothers womb in Psalm 139:13,15, and this infant is also meant to be a sacred dwelling place of God that no man has a right to terminate or destroy.

This second door shut out the court, but gave entrance to the priesthood for ministry in the holy place. The garments of Israel's high priest were made of the same material and colors as this door. In these garments he was a human tabernacle, a dwelling place of Yahweh, a holy place sanctified by His presence.

A sinner is quite safe to walk anywhere on earth, but to enter through this door into the holy place is only for those clothed with redeeming grace. As the tabernacle is a type of Christ, so also is this door a reminder that only through Him is entrance gained into this presence of God.

The *five pillars* that held up the door tell us it is by grace. They were made of acacia wood overlaid with gold; the humanity of Jesus overlaid with His deity. The five pillars each had chapiters, or *ornaments at the top* as though *crowned with glory and honor*, which is the testimony of the *five* writers of the epistles-Paul, Peter, John, James and Jude.

They testify there is a crown of *incorruptibility* (I Cor. 9:25) for those who remove the leaven of pride, hypocrisy and legalism.

There is a crown of *rejoicing* (I Thes. 2:19) for those who by their lives and testimony gain others to believe the gospel.

There is a crown of *righteousness* (II Tim.4:8) for those who live righteous lives, while they eagerly are expecting His return.

There is a crown of *life* (James 1:12) for those who are faithful in their testimony and life to a true representation of the gospel.

There is a crown of *glory* (I Pet. 5:4) for those who shepherd the flock of God by teaching, caring for and guiding them.

The term *pillars* is given to James, Peter and John, who gave the handshake of fellowship to Barnabas and Paul (Gal. 2:9). In Rev. 3:12, the *over comers are made pillars* "in the Temple (Naos) of My God."

The *sockets* under the pillars were of bronze, a type of judgment indicating that in spite of our privileged position, there still remains to be a judgment of ourselves and actions and motives. The *anointed of God still need correction*. And if we endure, we shall also reign with Him.

If "the saints will judge the world" (I Cor. 6:2), and "angels" (I Cor. 6:3), should we not learn how to judge among ourselves? "But if we judged ourselves rightly, we should not be judged" (I

Cor. 11:31). Much of the writing of the five authors has to do with correction and reproof and exhortation.

This serves as a constant reminder that the Jesus of which this door speaks and through which we gain entrance into the holy place stood Himself in the place of being judged and endured the cross on our behalf. He was at the same time the tabernacle in which God's presence dwelt and the tent in which He lived to be the meeting place for God and man. Apart from this mediator, even the believer can offer nothing that God can receive. Therefore we give thanks to the Father in the name of our Lord Jesus Christ.

The Veil

Ex. 26:31

The Only Way to The Father

Just prior to a week of silence with his friends, Job says to his wife, "Shall we indeed accept good from God and not accept adversity? In all this Job did not sin with his lips" (Job 2:10). At the end of the week of silence, "Job opened his mouth and cursed the day of his birth." (Job 3:1). "Why did I not die at birth?" (verse11). "Why is light given to a man whose way is hidden, and whom God has hedged in?" (verse 23).

In his book *The Gospel According to Job*, Mike Mason mentions how "God one day came to Job in a way he was not accustomed to" and that "faith and hope can reach a point of despair that is courageous, realistic and empowering. It can reach a point of abandonment, and is prepared to be deprived of sensual and psychological pleasure for the sake of holding out for deep spiritual truth."

Isaiah also had an experience like that. Though the two men were from different time periods and their encounters were dramatically different, the outcome seems to be similar. Isaiah says, "For my *eyes have seen* the King, the Lord of Hosts" (Isa. 6:5). Job says, "But now, *my eye sees* You" (Job 42:5 NKJV).

The object of our journey through the tabernacle is *to see* all the riches of God that are made available to us in Christ Jesus. But the *faith and hope that is courageous and realistic and persevering* will be a necessary part of our journey, also, as it was for Job and Isaiah.

Entering through the door into the holy place, we see on the right a small table with bread and incense. On the left, opposite the table, is a lamp stand with seven flames giving light. Beyond them is a small altar for burning incense just before the *veil*. This veil "shall be made with cherubim, the work of a skilful workman" (Ex. 26:31). And so it was made according to divine instruction (Ex. 25:40; 26:30; 27:8).

The expression *"the work of a skillful workman"* is used only in regards to the veil and the high priest's garments (Ex. 26:31, 28:6). Divine wisdom and skill were given to the workman to make these. This veil pointed to the humanity of Jesus, whose life was also in demonstration of the Father's skilful direction. The whiteness of the *pure linen* pointed to the sinless human nature of the Redeemer woven in God's loom. In Him the eyes of God could see every perfection of Himself, and this was demonstrated in a life of perfect obedience. "His fullness proved man's emptiness" writes A W Pink.

Hebrews 10:5, which says, "But a body You have prepared for me," gives us notice that Jesus in the flesh, represented in this beautiful veil made by skillful workman, was not plagued by sin as we are but pointed to His perfections instead. These perfections alone could be seen by the Father in the Holy of Holies. That's why the four pillars holding up the veil were behind it in the holy place. The veil was in effect a voice that said, "Do not enter past here." The *cherubim on the veil* provided the same warning as they did at the entrance to the Garden of Eden. There they guarded the perfections of God and made certain that man should not eat of Gods' eternal life until the sin problem was resolved.

The testimony of Jesus' life was that, *unless you are holy, sinless, spotless, and perfect* as He is, you cannot enter into the presence of God. He did not say there was no way, but that the way was being revealed before their eyes. "I am the way" (John 14:6). He fulfilled all the requirements necessary to satisfy His Father and as our substitute provided for us the way. The blood of substitution brought by the high priest through the veil and sprinkled on the mercy seat pointed forward to that.

This veil torn from top to bottom when Jesus said, "It is finished!" (John 19:30) declared that the way to God had now been made known. The way was now open for all who believe. That does not mean carnal flesh can now just march boldly into God's presence. *The veil was torn, but not removed.* Jesus is still the only way to the Father, and the cherubim testified of His judicial authority to judge everyone according to every word He had spoken (John 12:48).

The veil was made of the same linen and colors as the two previous entrances and the ceiling. In *the veil* (Ex. 26:31), the colors are mentioned first to emphasize the perfect humanity of Jesus by which man gains entrance.

In describing *the ceiling*, the fine twisted white linen is mentioned first (Ex. 26:1), and was predominate in order to point to the pure righteousness of the deity of Jesus under which the presence of God would dwell.

The veil was supported by *four pillars* made of acacia wood overlaid with gold, speaking again of the two natures of Christ. These pillars had *no decorative crown* at the top like the five at the entrance to the holy place.

The four Gospels tell the story of Isaiah's prophecy; "That He was *cut off* out of the land of the living, for the transgression of my people to whom the stroke was due" (Isa. 53:8).

Each pillar had *a golden hook* at the top, which held up the veil from above and put it on display. Jesus also was upheld by His Father from above while on earth below (John 8:29). The four gospel writers presented the perfections of Christ. In them we see the purple of His royalty and kingship; the scarlet red of the bleeding, suffering servant; the white of the righteous Son of Man; and the blue of the heavenly Son of God.

These pillars *rested on four silver sockets* made of the same atonement money used for making the sockets under the boards–the ransom Israel paid as its response to being the Redeemed people of God.

The Curtain Of Fine Linen

Ex. 26:1

God's Dwelling Place

In the holy of holies, God lived in the midst of Israel on the mercy seat of the ark between two Cherubim. They are the highest among the angelic order and minister God's judicial authority. On the veil before and on the curtain above the ark more cherubim were embroidered. Some name this curtain the *"mishkan"* which in Hebrew means "to dwell." It was God's *dwelling place, or Tabernacle,* as in Exodus 26:6. Others say this name refers to the boards. The word is used for a residence or dwelling, from hut, to tent, to temple.

This curtain with woven artistic designs of cherubim covered both the holy place and holy of holies, forming a sheltering canopy of protection. Not only did God surround Himself with cherubim, He also *provided this protection* for His people who ministered before Him in the holy place. "I will abide in your tabernacle forever; I will trust in the shelter of your wings" (Ps. 61:4, 91:4. NKJV).

In Revelation 7:15, there is a great multitude from every nation and all tribes and tongues before the throne. They came out of the great tribulation and they serve Him day and night in His temple (naos). And He who sits on the throne shall *"spread His tabernacle over them,"* NASB or "dwell among them" (NKJV).

This curtain was made of *fine linen* in *two sections* covering the holy place and the holy of holies. Each section consisted of *five curtains* that were 28 cubits long and 4 cubits wide, sown together at the edges. (1 cubit is about 50cm)

The *two sections of curtains* are like two sets of commandments.

The first five declare man's responsibility to God, and are joined together by the words, "The Lord your God" (Ex. 20:2). These, it can be said, cover and surround the holy of holies.

The second set of five commandments define man's responsibility to man, and do not contain the words "The Lord your God." These, it can be said, cover the holy place.

Ten is the number of human responsibility. In forming the ceiling with ten curtains, it is a picture of Christ as representing His people, fulfilling all the laws requirements and so satisfying the needs of God and man. For He alone loved God with all His heart, and His neighbor as Himself.

Where these two sections met over the veil, *50 blue loops* were attached to the two edges and were joined by *gold coupling.* (Ex. 26:5–6).

The number *fifty* speaks of the Holy Spirit poured out at Pentecost 50 days after His ascension. This Spirit was upon Him without measure and promised to all those who were to be born of Him.

The two sections joined together speak of Jesus being able to combine perfectly the claims of God and the needs of man.

Some examples would be His inflexible righteousness and great tenderness. He was uncompromising in faithfulness to His Father and abundant in compassion for poor sinners. He was stern in denouncing error and human traditions, yet very tender and patient toward those who were ignorant of Him. He displayed the authority of His Godhead and the meekness and lowliness of His manhood.

All these were seen to be united and combined in His life, just like these curtains were joined by *loops of blue* (heavenly grace) and *couplings of gold* (divine purity).

In His days on earth, many people saw Jesus only as *the bad-*

ger skin and as nothing that they desired. His presence served to reveal their blindness and hardness of heart. It aroused their enmity, having never seen past the wisdom of their pride, to see the mishkan's judicial authority.

But some, by the mercy and grace they had longed for and received "Beheld His glory, the glory as of the only begotten of the Father, full of grace and truth" (John 1:14).

They saw Him as the righteous one of God (the white), the Lord of Heaven (blue), the King of Kings (purple), and the suffering servant (scarlet). In this curtain, the white is mentioned first and is dominant.

For this inner curtain to be noticed, *one needs to look up* to Him who is now exalted and "crowned with glory and honor" (Heb. 2:7).

Inside, the priests could look up and see that God had "made foolish the wisdom of the world . . . Because the foolishness of God is wiser than men, and the weakness of God is stronger than men" (I Cor. 1:20, 25).

Isaiah, in chapter 5, describes a vineyard in which God was looking for *good grapes*. But he only found worthless ones. He was looking for justice and righteousness but found bloodshed and distress instead. Of the seven woes pronounced, the first six are applied to Israel.

Woe to those: who live for love of wealth (Isa.5:8), who live for the love of pleasure (verse 11), who live for love of iniquity (verse 18), who follow their theories and philosophies (verse 20), who follow their ego (verse 21), and who corrupt justice (verse 23). Each is a progressive step away from humility and trusting faith in God.

In chapter 6, Isaiah is now given to see a view of things that were above him and says, "I saw the Lord sitting on a throne *high and lifted up* . . ." and then pronounces the seventh woe upon himself. "Woe is me" (Isa. 6:1, 5 NKJV).

Stepping into the presence of God and beholding His glory is a humbling experience. It was for Isaiah and will be for us as well.

In the natural light of the outer court, we can see, criticize and point out with conviction the iniquity, ignorance and failures of others.

In the light of the Spirit of God and His Shekinah glory, we see not only our own filthy rags, but also the righteous perfections of Him in whose name we have come into the presence of God.

The "Ohel" Of Goats Hair

Ex. 26:7

The Meeting Place

The curtain of white linen was the first layer hung over the boards. The next layer was made of *black goat's hair* spun by the women of Israel (Ex. 35:26). This came from the same goat skins that were used for making their own tents. This curtain was called *ohel* in Hebrew, meaning it was clearly seen as a tent. As such it was *a meeting place* for His people (I Chron. 6:32).

This curtain is referred to as *tent over the tabernacle* in Ex. 26:7, or Ohel over the Mishkan. Moses was to join the two halves of the *tent* together (Ex. 26:11). So it was God's dwelling place (tabernacle) and Israel's meeting place (tent). The Hebrew (OT) uses these two distinct words. In the NT, John refers to Jesus in chapter 1:14 and writes, "The Word became flesh and *dwelt* among us." Meaning–to tent or encamp; to reside as God did in the tabernacle of old.

The *spun goat hair curtains* were of the same four cubits width as the linen, but were two cubits longer at 30 cubits. And instead of ten, there were *eleven*; five at the back, and six at the front. *Five* and *six* are the numbers of grace and man; God's grace coupled to man's need. These were joined over the veil, but now *bronze couplings* were used, which speaks of judgment. There is no mixing of goats with gold. Sin is always judged, never glorified.

The eleventh curtain draped down over the front entrance two cubits and doubled back up, so it was clearly *visible from the front.* Jesus also was made visible as the sin offering during the last 3 years of His 33-year life.

For those who entered the holy place, *this one eleventh* section was a reminder of the great cost paid by their Redeemer to provide entrance for them. This curtain pointed to Christ as the great sin offering for His people.

When Israel gathered for their seven annual feasts, *five* times the goat was the only animal used for the sin offering (Num. 28:16–29:40).

1) *The combined feast of Passover and unleavened bread and first fruits.*
2) *The feast of weeks (Pentecost).*
3) *The feast of trumpets.*
4) *The feast of Atonement. (The bullock was for the high priest and the priesthood. The goat and scapegoat were for the sin of the nation.)*
5) *The feast of Tabernacles.*

On *six* other occasions a goat was required for a sin offering.

1) *When a leader sins. Lev. 4:22.*
2) *When anyone of the common people sins. Lev. 4:27.*
3) *At the inauguration of the priest. Lev. 9:3.*
4) *At the inauguration of the tabernacle. Num. 7:16.*
5) *Failure in observing all that the Lord had commanded. Num. 15:24.*
6) *A sin offering at the beginning of each month. Num. 28:1–15.*

These combined make for a total of 11 occasions. God will abide where the sin issues have been dealt with.

The *goat* can be found in connection with sin and deception. In the story of Gen. 27 Rebekah, who loved Jacob, hears Isaac is about to give Esau his parting blessing. This blessing Rebekah wants for Jacob. Using *goat's* meat to entice Isaac and *goat's* hair to deceive him and Esau's clothes to fool his sense of smell, they are successful in obtaining the blessing for Jacob from Isaac. Twenty one years later, the deception still causes Jacob to fear for his life. The night before he is about to meet his brother Esau again, he wrestles with an angel saying, "I will not let you go unless you bless me." Gen. 32:26. The change of his name from "deceiver" or "trickster" to "one who persists with God" is quite a testimony of a changed life.

The inherent nature of sin passes from one generation to the next. His own descendents were jealous of his favoritism toward Joseph and sell their brother of dreams and coat of many colors to merchants on the way to Egypt. His colorful coat was dipped in *goat's* blood and presented to their father as their cover story for Joseph's death having been caused by a wild animal (Gen. 37:31). God's prevailing purpose was not to be thwarted by man's deception. The dreams of Joseph come literally true to life in Egypt. His royal robe as second in command over all Egypt demanded the subjection of everyone, including his brothers. His authority could now dictate that, "the man in whose hand the cup has been found, he shall be my slave" (Gen. 44:17). This is quite a remarkable statement by Joseph, who is also seen as a type of Christ, for the partakers of the communion cup also are understood to be declared as servants of the living God (John 13:16).

Not long after becoming Saul's son in law, David avoids being pinned to a wall by Saul's spear, and Michal recommends he leave by the window. She puts the household idol in bed and a quilt of *goat's hair* on its head, saying to Saul's messengers, David is sick. Later she tells her father that David threatened to kill her (I Sam. 19:11–17).

In each of these stories there is more than enough reason to bring a *goat* for a sin offering. But our subject is the goats hair covering, not the offering. So I will finish with an illustration Jesus used of goats.

In Matt. 25:33, Jesus is comparing sheep and *goats.* He is comparing the *goats* to those who did not recognize Him in those who were hungry and thirsty, who were strangers and naked and sick and in prison. Jesus not only sent His followers into the highways and byways to find them, He went there Himself. James writes that pure and undefiled religion is to visit orphans and widows in their distress. It is the great sin of pride in all mankind that fails to recognize Him in those whose lives appear to be absent of His blessing of prosperity. With these Jesus not only identified Himself, but he was also made to be sin for them. Those who know that of Him recognize Him in the Ohel covering of common goats hair as the meeting place for a needy people and a Holy God. In Him there is no deception. He qualifies to have our trust.

Rams Skins Dyed Red

Ex. 26:14

The Covering of Substitution

The "tabernacle" and "tent" curtains were covered over with red-dyed ram skins. These speak of Christ, as He *appeared to the eye of God*. In life He was God's faithful witness. In His death He was a substitute for man.

The ram was the only animal used on three different occasions.

1) As a *trespass offering* for a law broken by man (Lev. 5:15). It typified Jesus in restoration. He fully restored the honor of this broken law.

2) As the *burnt offering* at the consecration of the priests (Ex. 29:18, Lev. 8:18). It typified Him as being fully consecrated and surrendered to God's intended purpose in the place of man's failure to do so. In this was man's assured acceptance.

3) As an *offering for the ordination* of the priests to their office and authority. (Ex.9:19–22, Lev. 8:22). It typified Him in maintaining, leading and bearing the people's iniquity before God and His holiness before the people.

During His ministry on earth, Jesus was clearly seen as a *leader of His people*. His wisdom and teaching, demonstrated in mighty signs and miracles, would draw and influence great crowds of people. Yet He was willing to be forsaken by all and stand alone like a ram at the head of the flock, *accepting the responsibilities* of putting on display the holiness entrusted to Him.

Only hours before His crucifixion, Jesus prays to tell His

Father, "And for their sakes I sanctify Myself, that they them-selves also may be sanctified in truth" (John 17:19). This entire chapter tells of Jesus acknowledging the responsibilities given and entrusted to Him.

:2   You have given Him authority over all flesh,

:2 . . . He should give eternal life to as many as You have given Him.

:4 . . . I have finished the work You have given Me to do.

:6 . . . the men whom You have given Me out of this world.

:7 . . . all things which You have given me are from You.

:8 . . . For I have given them the words which You have given Me.

:11 . . . keep through Your name those whom You have given Me,

:12 . . . Those whom You gave Me I have kept.

:22 . . . And the glory which You gave Me I have given them, . . .

:24 . . . that they may behold My glory which You have given Me.

With all this given and entrusted to Him, we can be sure His prayer "that they may all be one, as You, Father, are in me, and I in You; that they also may be one of us . . ." (John 17:21 NKJV), will be answered. The Father will see to it. As our leader, sub-stitute and high priest, He lived not only and entirely for His Father, but He also died in obedience for man's sake. His prayer and testimony were sealed with His own blood. The red ram skins testify to this.

Let's look back again some 2000 years before the crucifixion at another aspect in the story of Abraham's life where God directs him to offer Isaac, his son of promise. As Abraham responds in faith and holiness to this divine order, Isaac asks a question. "Where is the lamb?" It is answered with, "God will provide for Himself a lamb." When Abraham's faith is fully tried and tested, he gratefully finds provided a ram in *substitution* for Isaac.

Abraham called the name of the place Yahweh Yireh in Hebrew, meaning "The Lord Will Provide." God was not just looking for an outward act from Abraham, but an inner state of surrender, a willingness to give up his beloved son to the care of his covenant God.

There were a series of experiences in Abraham's trail of faith that foreshadowed some of the great historical event of God the Father offering up His Son Jesus in *substitution* for the redemption of man.

1) Isaac was the *only son* according to the promise of God, who was loved. God knew, understood and even said that to Abraham. ". . . . your only son whom you love" (Gen 22:2). But then He also loved His own and only son. "For the Father loves the Son" (John 5:20). "For this reason the Father loves me, because I lay down My life that I may take it again" (John 10:17).

2) Abraham and Isaac were of one mind and purpose to go, worship and return: " . . . we will worship and return to you" (Gen 22:5). Jesus testified that He and the Father *were also one* in the plan of Redemption. "If I do not the works of My Father, do not believe Me; but if I do them . . . believe the works, that you may know and understand that the Father is in Me, and I in the Father" (John 10:37,38). "And . . . that they may be one just as We are one" (John 17:22).

It was Isaac who carried the wood, while Abraham carried the knife. It was Jesus who carried the cross, while the Father carried out the deadly sentence of judgment against sin.

3) Isaac and his father *walked together* (Gen 22:6). They agreed not only on the purpose of going but the way to go there. That's why Jesus could say, "I am the way, the truth, and the life . . . The words that I say to you I do not speak on My own initiative, but the Father abiding in me does His works" (John 14:6,10).

4) Abraham's faith testified of what he understood only God could provide. "*God will provide* for Himself the lamb" (Gen. 22:8), he said to Isaac. John the Baptist could point to Jesus and say, "Behold the Lamb of God that takes away the sins of the world" (John 1:29). Long centuries before this, Job's faith also could testify, "I know that my Redeemer lives" (Job 19:25).

5) Isaac was *willing* to be bound by his father (Gen. 22:9). He could have run away, but didn't. Instead he probably helped to build the altar. Jesus said, " . . . the Father knows Me and I know the Father; and I lay down my life for the sheep . . . No one has taken it from Me, but I lay it down on my own initiative" (John 10:15,18).

6) "In the mount of the Lord, *it will be provided*" (Gen. 22:14). Jesus had been there to observe Abraham's act of faith and could testify to Israel that "Your father Abraham rejoiced to see My day, and he saw it and was glad" (John 8:56). The mountain on which this event took place on was Moria, which is the place of the present day temple mount in Jerusalem. The city where Jesus was crucified, providing the needed substitution for our redemption. As *the Lamb* of God, He increased in favor with God and man. As *the ram*, the world hated Him for His testimony that its works were evil.

Badger Skins

Ex. 24:16

The Covering of Lowly Meekness

The Hebrew word for badger is "tachash" which is an animal with fur which some say refers to an antelope. Others say it is a member of the dolphin family. These have fins but no scales and would have been considered unclean and therefore unfit for the tabernacle. Either way, these badger skins portray Christ as He *appeared before men.*

In Eze. 16:10, these skins were used for making sandals. This tells of the lowliness and humility of Jesus, but also strength and durability of character.

This outer cover was not meant to display the holy perfections of Jesus seen by God in the fine linen inner curtain. God put on display that He dwelt with equal favor under the covering of Christ's glory and righteousness as well as the deep humility by which He put on the form of a man. In the peace offering, there was a similar message. Perfect pardon did not mean perfect holiness for sinful man, even though fellowship was restored with God.

I trust *God intended to present Jesus* as badger skins to display Him in humility and as approachable. To man He made Himself of no reputation, was born in a manger, was brought up in lowly Nazareth and worked as a carpenter. "As for this fellow, we know not from where He is" (John 9:29).

Isaiah 53 speaks of Him as having "no stately form or majesty that we should look upon Him. . . . He was despised and forsaken of men. A man of sorrows and acquainted with grief. And like one from whom men hide their face. He was despised and we esteemed Him not."

What an enormous contrast of Him is presented by God to man in just the four different layers that covered His dwelling place on earth. How prophetic was this portrayal.

He was the *perfect righteousness of God* in which the Shekinah glory would dwell among sinners.

Jesus was also the *meeting place* between all the pollution of sin on earth and the sinless perfection of heaven.

Then He was portrayed as the redeemer who would *substitute Himself for sinful man* and lead His redeemed people to restored glory.

And so it should not surprise us that God would portray Him as *lowly, humble, approachable and yet of enduring strength.*

Can someone present a model or a better way than what God chose to do through faith in His Son? What would better demonstrate the extent of God's love, His glory and humility, His grace and mercy, His power over kingdoms and principalities, and in contrast show the extent of our sin natures while leaving us as free moral agents, created in His image to respond to His invitation and let Him be Lord of our lives?

The tabernacle model has been with us for a long time. It has been our choice to ignore its message of a very comprehensive and succinct portrayal of the person and work of Christ.

God had committed to Jesus, 1) the work of creation and sustaining it; 2) the glory of His name; 3) the honor of His law; 4) the redemption of man; and 5) the sending of the Holy Spirit. It was his humility among other characteristics that made Him adequate for these. In Him there was no thought of setting Himself up above the throne of God as the pride of Lucifer had intended.

Just as there *are no dimensions* given for the outer two coverings, so there is *no dimension to the necessity of humility* for those to whom these things are now entrusted. The people of faith are the stewards of the creation. To them has been entrusted the glory of God and the honor of the moral law and of abiding in the Spirit of Christ. How little of this we comprehend.

In Mark 10:35, two of the disciples come to Jesus with a question. "Teacher, we want you to do for us whatever we ask you."

They may have remembered Jesus saying "that if two of you agree on earth about anything that they may ask, it shall be done for them by my Father who is in heaven" (Matt. 18:19).

They ask for a *nearness to the glory and power of Jesus*. "Grant that we may sit in Your glory, one on your right, and one on Your left."

That's a good request. We should all desire such nearness. But Jesus answers them with saying they don't know what they are asking.

Jesus speaks gently to our ignorance. Nearness to Him requires a willingness to drink from two cups–the cup of His blessing (I Cor. 10:16), which we all like, and the cup of His suffering, which we all like to avoid. The desire for being important, happy, holy, etc. usually has self at the heart of it.

The cup Jesus drank in the garden of Gethsemany took away the curse of God's wrath against our sin but not of suffering. Our Gethsemany still needs the *humble surrender* of our wills as part of the higher life of nearness, glory and power. A seed must fall into the ground and die to produce new life.

When Jesus asks them if they are able to drink this cup, they said, "We are able" (verse 39). Jesus accepts their word even though He knows they would all forsake Him. It would have been more truthful to say, "We believe to be able, but our unbelief needs your help to drink this cup."

The jealousy of the other disciples served to show they were just as unprepared for what was before them as the two. How often the seeking after holiness becomes a point of contention and division.

They had only seen in Jesus *more of their own likeness*. How little they had understood *of the other coverings* over the tabernacle. The humble appearance of badger skins had veiled their eyes to the mishkan of Jesus.

The Gold Covered Table

Ex. 25:23–30

For Communing and Securing

Jesus "did not enter a holy place made with hands, a mere copy of the true one, but into heaven itself" (Heb. 9:24). Should not then those who are born again as temples of God, also be made without hands, renewed by the Spirit of God and the word of God (Eph. 4:20–24), and so appear before Him?

Though the tabernacle of Moses was realized in Jesus, there remains great value in knowing for example, how in the many details displayed in the five different offerings at the altar, full and complete redemption was attained for man. They display far more information than the common statement, "Jesus died to save us." Added to that is the great gain in having our minds washed at the laver. It is also of great benefit to understand that the holy place bore witness to His ongoing work for us in heaven after His ascension. So the tabernacle is useful to lay a comprehensive understanding of the gospel.

Proceeding now into the holy place, only a few things were allowed to be brought in. These were the consecration of the priest; oil for the lamp stand; incense and fire for the altar; bread, wine and incense for the table; and on special occasions blood was brought in because of sin by the high priest or nation. Each of these items is a picture worth a thousand words.

It's helpful to understand the designated place, display and use of these items. They represented what Jesus brought to the Father on our behalf. We will take some time to examine these items, " . . . that we might know the things freely given to us by God" (I Cor. 2:12).

In describing the *table of bread*, God begins by saying, "you shall also make" (Ex. 25:23 NKJV). He had just finished describing to Moses the ark of the covenant with the words from Ex. 25:22, "There I will meet with you from above the mercy seat, from between the Cherubim."

It is one of two places in the description of the tabernacle that this phrase "also make" is used. The other is in Ex. 30:18. God is connecting the *place of His throne* to the place where *He communes* with His people at the table.

David does likewise in bringing Jonathan's son Mephibosheth to his table. David demonstrates his full *reconciliation* with this descendant of Saul by saying, "Mephibosheth shall eat bread at my table regularly" (II Sam. 9:10). It demonstrated that *the covenant between David and Jonathan* was being applied to Jonathan's son by bringing him into the place of close fellowship with the king.

The communion table in church is also a testimony that for those who own Jesus as Redeemer and King, there is a table of fellowship and reconciliation around which we all share of the same food.

While the ark and the mercy seat are a type of the throne of grace belonging to the King of Glory, it was not the place of communion.

"The mercy seat speaks of Jesus as the *basis of our fellowship*. The table points to Jesus as the *substance of our fellowship*. The food of God in whom we have communion with His people," writes A.W. Pink in his book *Gleanings in Exodus*.

A king may have an audience chamber (praetorium) and a throne room to receive subjects and from where he would distribute his honors and judgments. But it was not the place of fellowship. Fellowship implies common interest, dialogues and sharing of blessings.

In Ex. 24:11, there was a meal on Mount Sinai that celebrated the ratification of a covenant. "And they beheld God and they ate and drank." The same God of authority that had pronounced the law from the mountain was now having communion with His people.

This table in the tabernacle was small—*two cubits long*—and tells of the communion and agreement among God and His people. "Can two people walk together unless they be agreed" (Amos 3:3).

The *width of one cubit* tells of the one resurrected life sustaining us. "that He would grant you, according to the riches of His glory, to be strengthened with power through His Spirit in the inner man" (Eph. 3:1).

It had the *same height as the mercy seat of 1½ cubits*. God places His glory on the mercy seat at the same height as communion with His Son and those who abide in Him.

The ½ cubit would suggest that "we only know in part" (I Cor. 13:9). As the Queen of Sheba pointed out, "It was a true report that I heard in mine own land . . . and behold the half was not told me" (I Kings 10:7).

The table made of *wood overlaid with gold* tells again of Jesus being humanity in deity. It had *two crowns* of gold around the table top.

The inner crown speaks of Christ glorified. This crown was for keeping the bread on the table even during travel. As there were 12 cakes of bread representing the 12 tribes of Israel, it was the people of God who were maintained in the presence of God by the Christ who is "crowned with glory and honor" (Heb. 2:9).

Around this first crown was a margin of a hand breadth (about 23 cm.). So God's people are *secured by His glory* and *guarded by His hand*:" . . . no one shall snatch them out of My hand" (John 10:28).

The second crown tells of a further glory. A glory that God attaches to His name. "For My name's sake I will defer my anger" (Is. 48:9 NKJV). " . . . Do it for Your name's sake" (Jer. 14:7 NKJV).

The *glory of God's name is at stake* if He fails to secure His people in His presence and fulfill His promises.

Bread of the Presence

Lev. 24:5–9

Bread of Faces (Hebrew)

At the altar, we see Jesus in the finished work of redemption. There in His humiliation He secures for every believer by an everlasting covenant His ability " . . . to keep you from stumbling, and to make you stand in the presence of His glory blameless with great joy" (Jude 1:24)

In *the meal offering at the altar,* we see Jesus in His humiliation being ground like fine flour in all His work of obedience, love and service to man. There the fine flour testified to His trials, deep sorrow, temptations, and rejection by man on account of sin and hardness of heart. These sufferings did not make Him more perfect, but they made His perfections visible.

In *the bread of the presence on the table,* we see Him in resurrection glory as a memorial before God, representing His people. And as such He is the substance for restored communion with God.

The initial Sabbath rest was destroyed by man's fall into sin. But here at the table God assures His people by an everlasting covenant that *the rest will be restored.* This was testified to by the unleavened bread that was to be replaced every Sabbath (Lev. 24:8–9). It is an everlasting covenant for the sons of Israel. Every Sabbath is a memorial of eternal rest to come. Though the bread was changed, it always remained before the presence of God.

The same fine flour used for the cakes of the meal offering, was also used for making the loaves on the table. These loaves were all equal in size, testifying that before God there was equal representation of His people. The loaves were perforated even as Jesus was pierced.

The 12 loaves were each made of 2 omers of flour. This was a double portion of one's daily manna of one omer. There was here a portion of food for both God and the priest.

Two omers equal approximately 10 pints. If today a bread making machine uses 2 pints of flour to make a 1½ pound loaf of leavened bread, then each loaf of show bread would be about seven pounds.

Perhaps God Himself joined Aaron and his two sons to eat the abundance of bread as He did with Abraham (Gen. 18:8).

In Lev. 24:8–9, it does say that it was eaten by the priesthood in the holy place in the presence of God. So this bread was not only for the Father's delight, but also for those who have come into His presence.

Jesus was also the *delight* of God and man. At Jesus' baptism, the Father spoke of His Son as one, "in whom He had *great delight*" (Luke 3:22). Isaiah 42:1 prophesies of this Servant as "My chosen one in whom *My soul delights*." Is the condition of our heart and mind such that this delight is true for us? Is the resurrected Jesus the food of our delight? There appears to be an endless array of other things that competes for it. *The blame of our hunger for God will never be for lack of God's provision.*

Paul writes to the Corinthians of the Lord's table (I Cor. 10:21) and the Lord's supper (I Cor. 11:20). *Both are His.* But the first would indicate to whom and how we come. The second gives the reason for coming. It is similar with the table and the show bread. The table tells of Jesus as the *sustainer of our relationship.* The bread tells of *the substance* of our relationship. Is our relationship with Jesus sustaining and delightful?

Pure frankincense is made from gum which is very white. This was placed "on each row" (Lev. 24:7) of loaves to express the fragrance and purity of character seen in all His ways, actions and thoughts. He was this not because He was separated from any nearness to sinful man. It was in demonstration of His own sinless nature.

There was no mistrust or murmur or suspicion in His heart toward God. He had no double minded intentions that said one thing and did another. Everything was the spontaneous exhibition of Himself. His ways were white and pure like frankincense. *What Jesus endured* was typified by the fine flour. *The character Jesus exhibited* was represented by pure frankincense. Upon both of these the Father's eye rested with delight.

The *gold spoons* were for carrying about a handful of frankincense.

The *jars* (Ex. 25:29) were for pouring out libation offerings. "In the holy place you shall pour out a libation offering of strong drink to the Lord" (Num. 28:7). When an Israelite brought a burnt offering with a meal offering and drink offering, it was brought to the altar of sacrifice, and the drink offering was poured out at the altar to express the worshipper's hearty concurrence in all that he saw at the altar.

When the priest brought burnt and meal offerings on Sabbaths, new moons and appointed feasts for corporate Israel, the accompanying drink offerings were poured out in the holy place as evidence of God's acceptance.

The *dishes* were made of pure gold and were simple vessels for holding food. Some think these dishes and spoons and jars and covers were laid out in the margin around the table between the two crowns.

For six days these would be a silent witness that on the seventh day the bread on the table would be placed on them.

The hymn "Bread of heaven feed me 'til I want to more," is a testimony that there is a bread in heaven which is Jesus, the bread of life.

The Syrophoenician woman's dish was empty, but she came believing she would be fed, and Jesus answered her, "Oh woman, your faith is great. Be it done for you as you wish" (Matt. 15:27).

"Manna" "Bread of Life" "Bread of the Presence"

John 6:49; John 6:35; Luke 24:30–31.

Abundant Supply

When Jesus was introduced into the human race, He came into the midst of a national mindset with some very mistaken expectations about the coming Messianic Kingdom. They expected a kingdom of strength and wealth, which would make life better for them. People of all nations follow after heroes, idols and gods to improve their lives.

When Jesus began healing the sick, raising the dead, making the blind see, the lame to walk, and feeding a crowd, then a lot of problems were solved for those people. They had many more problems that needed fixing to make life better and easier.

So it is understandable that they wanted to take Jesus by force and make Him King (John 6:15). It is not surprising that they said, "Lord, evermore give us this bread which comes down out of heaven" (John 6:33).

We all like subjective experiences where real felt needs are realized and life becomes better and easier. But these were not meant to be elevated above God's intended purpose. We are not to ignore the veils which God put between our sight and the unseen. Of these He removes no more than is necessary to reveal what needs to be sanctified.

If Jesus had healed everyone, had driven out all the Romans, had fed all the needy and had set Himself on a throne, how long would Israel have followed Him? Was He not already their King? Their Savior? Their Prophet? Their Priest? Were their own percdived needs so great that they could not recognize the Kingdom of Heaven that stood in their midst? *If Jesus as He is, is not attractive, is it possible that He has not been received as Savior? By them or us!* For us also, "there is no other name under heaven that has been given among men by which we must be saved" (Acts 4:12). The gospel will always be foolish to the unbeliever (I Cor. 1:23). "Behold I lay in Zion a stone of stumbling to the disobedient and a rock of offence" (Rom. 9:33).

Why were so many in history past willing to be beaten and imprisoned for believing, while multitudes just wanted something that made life better and easier for themselves?

It's because God provides different kinds of food. There is a *food for the body*, which perishes, even though it sustains life for a time. There is a *food for the mind*, which transforms it to enduring eternal life (John 6:27). And there is *a food for the inner man*, provided by His presence and nearness.

The *food for the body* is seen in the daily manna which foreshadowed Christ as the food for His Pilgrim people. "Your fathers ate the manna in the wilderness, and they died" (John 6:49). Not unlike common grace that sustains us all.

And then He provides a food for the mind which is the true bread from heaven (John 6:32). Six times Jesus refers to being *bread from heaven*. "The bread . . . which I shall give for the life of the world is my flesh" (verse 51). Jesus responds to their argument in verse 52 in the aorist tense, meaning a once for all action. "He who eats my flesh and drinks my blood has eternal life" (John 6:54). Jesus is not speaking of communion. It does not save. It is a repeated act of remembrance, where Jesus uses the word body, not flesh.

The issue is *about believing* "in Him whom He has sent" (John 6:29), and *receiving* "the Spirit who gives life" (verse 63). He wanted them to believe that "He was in the beginning with God and (that He) the Word was God" (John 1:1). And "the Word became flesh and dwelt among us" (John 1:14).

He continues. "Unless you eat the flesh of the Son of Man *(believe in the word that became flesh),* and drink His blood, *(drink of His life giving Spirit–receive the Spirit's witness)* you have no life in yourself" (verse 53).

John the Baptist had testified to this also in John 3. "He who comes from above is above all" (verse 31). "For He whom God has sent speaks the words of God" (verse 34). *Believe this.* Eat the word that became flesh. "For He gives the Spirit without measure" (verse 34). *Receive this Spirit.*

They concluded that Jesus was making a difficult statement (John 6:60), and they walked with Him no more.

Jesus, the Laver, had sought to renew their minds by washing them with His Word. His answers would fix the problems of their *anxiety, fear, doubt, and unbelief* so they could eat of the bread of the presence.

The answers they wanted were for a change of circumstances. So they left.

There were others like Peter and the disciples who believed and testified saying, "You have *words of eternal life*" (verse 68).

These *words of life* were also spoken by Jesus to two disappointed followers on the road to Emmaus. He "explained to them the things concerning Himself in the Scriptures . . . in the law of Moses and the Prophets and the Psalms" (Luke 24:27,44). It impacted them deeply. "Were not our hearts burning within us while He was explaining the scripture?" (verse 32).

While reclining at their table, "He took the bread and blessed it, and breaking it, He began giving it to them. And their eyes were opened and they recognized Him" (verse 31).

This bread of the presence, or *"bread of faces," is for those whose hearts burn within them* (verse 32). They had been fed at the table of His presence, and they went out singing a new song to others. Those who do not receive the Word do not receive of His presence. This bread is for those of the royal priesthood who want more than just to eat of His manna and testimony. They also want to be renewed by His nearness.

In Remembrance Of Me

Matt. 26:28; Luke 22:20; I Cor.11:25.

The Covenant of Communion

A covenant, like marriage, is a solemn transaction between individuals or nations or at times between God and man where each party is bound to fulfill the conditions and obligations agreed to. The expectations of covenant promises made by the prophets had just been clarified by John the Baptist (John 1:19–34), when a voice from heaven said of Jesus at His baptism, "This is My beloved Son in whom I am well pleased" (Matt. 3:17). Jesus accepted the implications of His Father's voice and was led into a wilderness to be tested on this. Jesus entered this time of severe temptation *full* of the Holy Spirit (Luke 4:1), but He left it *full of the power* of the Holy Spirit (Luke 4:14). This empowerment by wilderness experience was meant to become one of many benefits the lives of His covenant people would be privileged to demonstrate (Acts 3:12).

Just before this empowerment of oneness Jesus enjoyed with His Father was to be tested one last time, He took a cup at the last supper, gave it to His disciples and said, "this cup which is poured out for you, *is the new covenant in My blood*" (Luke 22:20), "drink from it, all of you" (Math. 26:27). Of His life and covenant union with the Father they were from now on to drink.

In being the originator of covenants, He was well acquainted with the implications and powerful influences of its promises, requirements and commitments. These existed between His Father, Himself and His people.

In I Sam. 18:3 we find stated the principle reason for a covenant.

"Then Jonathan made/cut a covenant with David because he loved him as himself."

Was this not the reason God had established His everlasting covenant with Adam, (Gen. 3:15), Noah, (Gen 9:12), Abram, (Gen. 15:18), and Israel? (Jer. 31:36). His promise was never maybe. He was the "I am that I am." Every deed and word that flowed from His own life was in keeping with His covenant.

What requirements, benefits and responsibilities were His followers now included in as they were seated around the communion table? Let's start with Abram when he returns from liberating Lot. Melchizidek brings bread, wine and a blessing to Abram saying, "Blessed be Abram of God Most High, Possessor of heaven and earth" (Gen. 14:19). A remarkable declaration–Abram belongs to and is owned by God as heaven and earth are. "And blessed be God most high who has delivered your enemies into your hands."

Abram *recognizes* the bread, wine and blessings as symbols of a covenant offer. He also *receives* Melchizidek, King of Salem, as priest of God most High. And then Abram *accepts* the covenant and its *first* requirement in the terms that had been stated–*God owns and blesses Abram*. He then responds with the *second* requirement of *complete submission* by the giving of a "tenth of all" to Melchizidek.

That Abram made a covenant is evidenced by saying, "I have *sworn to the Lord God most High*, possessor of heaven and earth . . . lest you say, I have made Abram rich" (Gen. 14:23). Abram was not looking for a backup system should God fail. In this declaration we see the *3rd* requirement–*complete trust* that led to a life of extreme obedience and extravagant love.

In the making and cutting of a covenant, there was also a series of exchanges. The following references are a brief summary.

In Gen.15:17–*an exchange of places.* The flaming torch passes through between the halves of the animals, indicating that God was exchanging places with Abram. His need to know in verse 2 is exchanged for God's ability to provide. Abram was given the position of access to all of God's resources.

In Gen. 17:5,15–*an exchange of names.* The silent H sound of God's unpronounced name JHWH is now included in the name of Abram who became Abraham and Sarai who became Sarah. As follower of Christ, my name now includes "Christian."

In I Sam. 18:4–*an exchange of robes.* Jonathan, as heir to the throne, gives his royal robe to David, making David the next rightful heir to the throne of Israel. Think of how Jesus gave His robe of righteousness in exchange for our robe of sin.

In I Sam. 18:4–*an exchange of armor.* This provided the ability to fight offensively (the bow) and defensively (the sword). The means to do it was carried by the belt including the money bag. "Put on the whole armor of God that you may be able to stand firm" (Eph. 6:12).

In II Sam. 9:3–*an exchange of responsibility*. David was responsible for the descendants of Jonathan. "I will show kindness to you for the sake of your father Jonathan" (II Sam. 9:7). A beautiful picture of how God's wondrous grace is showing kindness to those who belong to the house of His enemies. He does that for Jesus' sake.

In II Sam.9:7–*an exchange of tables.* David makes a place for Mephibosheth at his own table and says " . . . you shall eat at my table regularly" Jesus promised this to his followers also saying, "I say unto you that He shall gird Himself and make them to sit down and eat and will come and serve them" (Luke 12:37).

. In II Sam 9:11–*an exchange of fellowship.* Mephibosheth went from servant in hiding to fellowship with the king

These are privileges and responsibilities of those enter into a covenant relationship with Jesus. Who accept the Lordship of

Jesus over their life; who, as members of Christ, remember His broken body as the evidence of God's holy wrath against their sin now being satisfied; and who remember His blood, which as evidence of the perfect life it represents, is God's means of bringing us into the new covenant of restored fellowship with Him and empowerment by Him.

The Golden Lampstand

Ex. 25:31

The "Menorah," Meaning "Light Bearer"

Jesus coming to earth and making Himself of no reputation does not mean He made Himself of no effect. In His humiliation He gave up His heavenly glory and self-existence. and for a time, was dependant and subject to an earthly father and mother. "Though He was rich, yet for your sakes he became poor that through His poverty you might become rich" (II Cor. 8:9).

He borrowed loaves and fishes to feed a multitude, borrowed a donkey to ride into Jerusalem, borrowed a boat to cross the Lake, a stable for His birthplace, an upper room for His last meal, a tomb for His grave, yet He was the light of the world in the middle of Israel.

When He began His public ministry, the light that had been in the tabernacle and temple for some 1440 years came out of the holy place and *became visible for the first time* to all of Israel. For He said:

> "We must work the works of Him that sent Me, as long as it is day; . . . While I am in the world, I am the light of the world"–John 9:4–5.

> "For a little while longer the light is among you . . . While you have the light, believe in the light, in order that you may become sons of *light*"–John 12:35,36.

"And this is the judgment, that the light is come into the world and men loved the darkness rather than the light; for their deeds were evil"–John 3:19.

It was not only Israel that rejected the light. So did the Romans and the Greeks. At the crucifixion, they thought they had extinguished this bright light that had penetrated uncomfortably deep into their darkness. But this light now dwells in the heavenly tabernacle. There the royal priesthood has constant access to Him.

The lamp stand typified *Christ as the Light* in the holy place. Its position was on the south side, opposite the table of bread, in a place of communion for the priesthood and ministry by them before God.

The three items located there each represented a form of fellowship. A.W. Pink mentions in his book, *Gleanings in Exodus* that: the table pointed to "*Christ as the substance of our fellowship,*" as the one in whom we are strengthened and have our delight; the lampstand pointed to "*Christ as the power of our fellowship*" as He empowers us in appointed ministries, according to gifts supplied; the altar of incense points to "*Christ as maintaining our fellowship*" through His work of intercession; the ark of the covenant points to "*Christ as the basis of our fellowship*" by means of the blood stained mercy seat in the holy of holies.

Everything in the holy place is done in the light of the lamp stand. Christ's ultimate goal is to bring us into the full fellowship of the Father. Being drawn into His righteousness was only the first step.

Saving us from sin by redemption and sanctifying us by His Word were necessary for coming into the holy place for fellowship. But here, also, His work continues until He has illuminated every step we need to take into the presence of the Father.

At the table we are to feed on Him and delight and abide

in Him and His resurrection life—*to be impressed by Him*. At the lamp stand we are anointed by Him with gifts and ministry and empowerment *to express ourselves about Him* to others as the light of the world.

At the table we learn from Jesus how *to love the Lord our God* with all our heart, soul, mind and strength. At the lamp stand we learn from Jesus *how to love and minister to our neighbors* as we do to ourselves.

In the Amplified version of Heb. 1:3, we read of Jesus that:

> "He is the sole expression of the glory of God, [the Light Being; the out raying or radiance of the Divine], and He is the perfect imprint and very image of [God's] nature, upholding and maintaining and guiding and propelling the universe by His mighty work of power."

"And he (Moses) lighted the lamps before the Lord."—Ex. 40:25.

This light of the lamp stand was *cast before the Lord*. The first concern of Jesus was His Father's glory. "Father glorify Your name" (John 12:28 NKJV).

The seven lamps radiated the *light upon Christ Himself* so that the believer can enjoy the perfections of God.

For many who have believed, Jesus will only be known as a suffering substitute for their sin. But those who assume the privileges and responsibilities of becoming priests of God, will see a revelation of Christ in the holy place far exceeding that of the altar of sacrifice.

The light was *cast upon the lamp stand itself* (Ex. 25:37). The light of this very elaborate lamp stand as a type of the Light of the world was to reveal its own beauty. It was a dark night when Judas went out to betray Him that Jesus said, "Now is the Son of Man glorified . . ." (John 13:31). It would have made more sense if Jesus had said that on the mount of transfiguration.

The light was *also for the table of bread.* The priesthood ate the bread of the presence in the light of the lamp stand, because "in Him, there is no darkness" (I John 1:5).

The lamp stand was *to cast its light upon the altar of incense.* Here Christ is typified as our intercessor, indicating that the effect of the light shining into the darkness depends on the work of intercession.

The kind of intercession represented here is for those who are light bearers in this world–those with whom the Father is "well pleased" and who are in union with Him and His work. Their testimony and work and praying is only done in the light of His glory and grace.

A Hammered Work

Ex. 25:18,31.

Into the Image of Christ

Under the enabling wisdom and skill and gifting of God, Beza-lel and Oholiab formed the Lamp stand out of a talent of pure gold. Elaborate in detail and fine workmanship, it was made by a process of hammering. The mercy seat and cherubim were also made this way.

To make a mold for a casting takes time and thought and skill. Once it is made, replicas are easily reproduced. Religions and things that are idolatrous or according to man's carnal mind can easily be cast into a mould and reproduced. Not so with the mind of Christ. Attributes such as holiness, purity, humility, and perfection can never be reproduced by pouring a life into a mould such as Aaron's calf.

Dimensions are not given. The glory and perfections and purity of Jesus are without limit or dimension. Its base is not described because the focus is on the stem, its branches and ornamentation, pure olive oil, pure light, pure gold, and wicks made of the linen robes of the priests. All were a type of Jesus' life.

The workmanship was a picture of the skill and wisdom of God who fashioned both the work of Christ and all those who were redeemed throughout the ages. It was a demonstration and display of God's deeper thoughts and higher ways.

The glory and attractions of Jesus' life and ministry were made visible by the same process that made the Lamp stand. As it was *formed by beating and hammering* outside the camp, so also Jesus was rejected and beaten, not in heaven, but on earth, as Isaiah 53:10 describes it.

Think of the process of forming the lampstand. How exact proportions had to be *hammered out of the talent of gold* for its base, stem and branches with its bulbs, flowers and fruit. It had to be according to the pattern shown by God to Moses. It was very important to have this image clearly in mind so the hammering would be in the right place for the right proportions of the stems and branches with their cups, bulbs and flowers.

Now try to think of what the Father had in mind during all the circumstances and events of Jesus life. How in every response to temptation, rejection, unbelief, teaching, healing, discipling, etc., He was found to be conformed and acting according to His Father's intent and purpose. As such He was a light that shines in the darkness.

Every act of obedience was another act of conforming the "Light Bearer" to become the one great glorious light that was a perfect reflection of "The One forming light" (Isa. 45:7). "He learned obedience through the things He suffered" (Heb. 5:8).

Many saw in Him only more of the same darkness that they themselves lived in. He was rejected by His brothers, scoffed at by His countrymen and hated by the religious establishment. He was tested from the wilderness to the cross. But here is what *the Father in heaven saw:*

"The holy offspring shall be called the Son of God"–Luke 1:35.

"A light to bring revelation to the Gentiles, and the Glory of Your people Israel"–Luke 2:32 (NKJV).

"You are my beloved Son, in you I am well pleased"–Luke 3:22 (NKJV).

"This is my beloved Son. Listen to Him"–(Mark 9:7).

Nicodemus was mystified. "How can these things be?" (John 3:9). The Jewish people argued, "How can this man give us His flesh to eat?" (John 6:52). The blind man testified, "How can a man who is a sinner perform such signs?" (John 9:16). The religious officers were impressed. "Never did a man speak the way this man speaks" (John 7:46). At the interrogation, Pilate concluded, "I find no guilt in this man" (Luke 23:4).

In His death *He destroyed the penalty of sin.* "If any man eats of this bread he shall live forever" (John 6:51). In His resurrection, *He destroyed the power of sin.* "Oh death, where is your victory? Oh death, where is your sting?" (I Cor. 15:55). In His ascension, *He destroyed the pollution of sin.* "The trumpet will sound and the dead will be raised imperishable" (I Cor. 15:52).

And what does God think of us who have been entrusted to be light bearers to our generation? *What did God see in us* before we even came to Christ? God saw in us who believe all the perfections of His Son. "He chose us in Him before the foundation of the world that we should be holy and blameless before Him" (Eph. 1:4), "according to the kind intention of His will" (verse 5), "according to the riches of His grace" (verse 7).

We are not an afterthought.

> "For You formed my inward parts; You covered me in my mother's womb. I will praise You, for I am fearfully and wonderfully made; Marvelous are Your works, And that my soul knows very well. My frame was not hidden from You, when I was made in secret, and skillfully wrought in the lowest parts of the earth. Your eyes saw my substance, being yet unformed, And in Your book they were all written, The days fashioned for me, When as yet there were none of them. How precious also are Your thoughts to me, Oh God."–(Ps. 139:13–17 NKJV).

David could write this about himself, but it can also be applied to the Christ in His humanity. And it is true of us as God sees us in union with His Son.

The events of our lives are also carefully orchestrated to *form and hammer us into a vessel of beauty* that upholds the Light of the World. The hammer that nailed Jesus to the cross is in my hand. The hammer that conforms me to His image as a lampstand is in His hand.

> "But we all with unveiled face beholding as in a mirror the glory of the Lord, are being transformed into the same image from glory to glory, just as from the Lord, the Spirit."–2 Cor. 3:18.

The Almond

Ex. 25:33

The Bud, Flower And Fruit

Becoming the first theocratic nation under the leadership of Moses at Mount Horeb was quite an awakening for Israel in 1440 BC.

The Almond tree is also the first tree to come to life after winter at the end of January. It is the first to bud flower and bear fruit, before even the leaves appear and before any other tree shows signs of life. Sometimes it is referred to as the awakening tree.

The Hebrew word for Almond is *Shaqad* which means, to be shaped like the almond. Another use of the word is to express being vigilant, alert, as for example in expecting God to fulfill His promises.

It was during Israel's formation as a nation that there was a rebellion contesting the leadership of Moses and Aaron. God settled the issue by first opening the earth to swallow up the rebellion of Korah and the 250 who joined him (Num. 16:1–2, 32). The next day after more accusations against Moses (verse 41), 14,700 died in a plague.

After this, God called for a rod from each of the twelve tribes, with their names written on them, to be laid in the tent of meeting in front of the ark (Num. 7:4). The following morning, *the rod of Aaron* had produced buds, flowers and ripe almonds (verse 8). *The buds* were symbols of new life, *the blossoms* were as symbols of beauty of character, and *the ripe almonds* were symbols of a fruitful life of purpose and usefulness like good tasting fruit.

This validated Aaron as the one to minister the life of Christ to Israel, and his rod was placed in the ark of the covenant.

Fourteen hundred and forty years later, Jesus Himself became that rod, and He ministered His own life to Israel.

Thirty-three years after His birth, there was another rebel lion and the "rod out of the stem of Jesse" (Isa. 11:1 KJV) (the almond branch) was "cut off" (Dan.9:26) at Calvary and buried (laid before God) (Luke 23:53). Three days later, He arose full of life, beauty and fruit (Acts 2:24, 41) as the bud, blossom and fruit of resurrected life.

This signified, "that under heaven no other name (high priest) was given by which we must be saved" (Acts 4:12).

It was these *buds, blossoms and almond fruit* that ornamented the stem and branches of the lamp stand. In Ex. 25:31 they are named as cups, bulbs and flowers. There were three sets in each branch for all the six branches and four in the center vertical stem for a *total of 22 sets* of the buds, flowers and fruit.

On the real almond tree, the bud appears first, then the flower, and in its place, the fruit. After this the leaves appear.

On Aaron's rod and the Lamp stand, all three—bud, flower, and fruit—were *found simultaneously*, signifying we do not need to discard the bud of new life, love joy emotions, etc. for the blossoms of the beauty of character or the usefulness of service. These can be and ought to be present simultaneously since we are ever receiving out of the fullness of the vine.

There may be a further testimony to this triple ornamentation.

In Psalm 19 we have in the first six verses a testimony of creation that is called a *general revelation* through which we can know God (Rom. 1:20), Like *the bud* appearing, to indicate new life.

In verses 7–11 there is a much more *specific revelation* in the Word of God and has more specific impact (Acts 6:7). This is like a *flower or blossom* giving a more beautiful and specific testimony of fruit to come.

Verses 12–14 testify of the *work of the Spirit* of God as He reveals errors, and hidden faults and presumptuous sins, etc. with the intent of producing a fruitful life (Gal. 5:22). This is like the beauty of blossoms turning to *fruit* on a tree.

These three levels of revelation can be illustrated another way. Think of the evidences at the resurrection.

Think of the *bud* as indicating a general revelation. Here the women found the stone was rolled away (Luke 24:2); they found tomb to be empty (verse 3); the linen clothes were lying in order (John 20:5); and the face cloth lying by itself (John 20:7). There is no sign of struggle and no voice, but still a witness that Jesus had risen from the dead.

Think of the *flower* as the specific revelation. Here an angel had rolled the stone away and sat on it (Matt. 28:2). There was a young man sitting at the right side (Mark 16:5–6), and two angels stood near the women (Luke 24:4). Then there were two angels sitting in the tomb who spoke to Mary (John 20:12–13). Now there was an angelic witness, a voice, as a more complete revelation that answered Mary's concern, "They have taken away my Lord and I do not know where they have laid Him."

Think of the *almond fruit* as the spirit revelation. Here Jesus makes His own personal appearances to the two disciples on the road to Emmaus (Luke 24:15) at the sea of Tiberias while they were fishing (John 21:1) and somewhere in Galilee (Matt. 28:10). They now had their own encounters with Him, they heard Him, and they saw Him eat.

The bud indicating a new life had come from an empty grave, which gave way to the flower of a more glorious angelic revelation, and the flower gave way to the fruit of resurrection testimony and personal encounter.

Those who have tasted of the fruit should not sit in judgment on those who see only the bud or the flower.

Those who have only seen the bud should not reject the testimony of those who have tasted the fruit.

The Lampstand of "Seven Lamps"

Ex. 25:37

The Seven Spirits of God

The seven lamps of the lamp stand gave *one light*. Yet this one light could be broken into its *seven varied colors*. As the bud of the almond testified of flower and the fruit to come, so did this one natural light before the Lord in the Holy place testify of a light in Heaven.

It also pointed to the *light of the seven Spirits* that are before the throne of God. "And there were seven lamps of fire burning before the throne of God which are the seven Spirits of God" (Rev. 4:5). These are identified in Isaiah 11:2. They correspond not only with the Lamp stand, but also *seven different components* of the Tabernacle. (See next page)

There is *a third* form of the light, where the Spirit takes of Jesus, "the light of world" and *distributes it to each of the members of His body,* the church. This is to empower their lives with gifts and ministries and continue on being a light in this world.

In I Cor. 12:4–6, Paul writes, "there are *varieties of gifts*, but the same Spirit" (verse 4) It is the Spirit that *gives* them. "There are *varieties of ministries* and the same Lord" (verse 5). It is the Lord that *directs* them. There are *varieties of effects*, but the same God who works all things in all persons." (verse 6). It is the Father that *empowers* them.

In his letters to the different churches, Paul mentions a variety of gifts in use or distributed throughout the church. In Rom. 12:6–8, we find 1) prophesy 2) service 3) teaching 4) encouragement 5) giving 6) leadership and 7) mercy. In I Cor. 12:4–11, he adds 8) wisdom 9) knowledge 10) faith 11) healing 12) miracles 13) discernment 14) tongues and 15) interpretation. In 1 Cor.12:28–30, he adds 16) apostleship 17) help and 18) administration. In Eph. 4:11, he adds 19) evangelism and 20) pastoring. In I Cor. 7:7, he adds 21) celibacy, and Peter adds 22) hospitality in I Pet. 4:9–11.

As there were 22 sets of almond buds, flowers and fruit on the lamp stand, so there are 22 gifts mentioned above. Gifts such as wisdom, knowledge and discernment *enable us "to know."* Gifts such as service, help, and hospitality *enable us "to do."* Gifts such as prophesy, teaching, and evangelism *enable us "to speak."*

Their purpose was to strengthen and edify the church; to extend the church's witness and ministry. They were not given for self-edification.

It illustrates that this one body has many parts. There is great diversity in unity and interdependence in diversity. And *unless the gifts are enacted in love,* "I contribute nothing" (I Cor. 13:1), "I am nothing" (verse 2) and "it profits me nothing"(verse 3).

The other meaning in Hebrew for the word *Almond* is to be "alert," "vigilant," or "expecting." These should be applied to the exercise of our gifts and ministry and the promises of God.

Lampstand	The Seven Spirits	Tabernacle Application
Center Stem	**The Spirit of the Lord**	**Ark of the Covenant** The presence of the Lord lived on the blood stained mercy seat and was guardian of the law.
First Pair of Branches	**The Spirit of Wisdom** and	**Gate of Repentance** By His doing you are in Christ Jesus who became to us wisdom from God
	Understanding	**Altar of Redemption** To understand the complete and finished work of our redemption. Washed by blood. Saved by grace through faith.
Second Pair of Branches	**The Spirit of Council** and	**Laver of Sanctification** The Word that councils, instructs, guides, corrects, washes and renews our minds.
	Strength	**Table of Bread** Delighting in Jesus the bread from heaven on which we feed. Strengthened by His Presence and secured by His Glory and name. The Place of our fellowship and union in the person of Christ.
Third pair of Branches	**The Spirit of Knowledge** and	**Lampstand of light** Abiding in Jesus, the light from heaven in which we walk. Knowing the gift of the Spirit, the ministry of the Son, the empowerment of the Father. The place of our fellowship and union in the body of believers.
	Fear of the Lord	**Altar of Incense** To pray with brokenness for the lostness of man. Appeal to the character of God from the depth of our hearts. Persist in prayer with the humility of Christ.

233

Oil of Beaten Olives

Ex. 27:21, 30:7–8

For the Lamp Stand

Lev. 24 1–4

Inside the holy place it was one of the duties of the priest to keep the lamp stand supplied with oil for the light (Lev. 24:3). It was Israel's duty to provide pure oil of beaten olives (Lev. 24:2). "Aaron and his sons shall keep it on order from evening to morning before the Lord" (Ex. 27:21). Meaning, the wicks trimmed, the oil was supplied to the cups, and the lamps were lit to burn all night. They were to trim the wicks *every morning* (Ex. 30:7), and light the wicks *every evening* (Ex. 30:8).

Oil was extracted from olives by two means. The first was by *crushing or beating.* This released the first outburst of pure, clear oil. The second method for extracting the remaining oil was by putting the pulp into a *press and squeezing* the oil out. This was never used in the holy place.

The beating of the olives is not unlike the beating of gold that formed the Lamp stand. Every strike on the gold was measured and directed to conform it to the intended shape. The olives also were beaten or crushed (if there was a crusher) so that only the pure oil was released. Each strike brought a *new spontaneous release of oil.*

Every act of rejection, unbelief, hostility, ignorance, pride, legalism, hypocrisy etc., released in Jesus a new flow of the Holy Spirit to the point of weeping over Jerusalem and sweating drops of blood. That's what made Him the light of the world.

Only what was pure Holy Spirit flowed from Him in His life and testimony. Not some natural talent or benevolence that He put on display to attract attention to Himself.

In our lives also, as representatives of Christ, it is the *pure beaten olive oil that needs to fuel our light*, not human talent or even the gift of the Holy Spirit. The people in Matt. 7:21 made that mistake. Their focus was revealed when they asked, "Did we not prophesy in Your name, and in Your name cast out demons, and in Your name perform many miracles?" This was a conscious expression of the pride of self. The people in Matt. 25:37 said, "When did we see You hungry and feed You or thirsty and give You drink?" Here was an unconscious manifestation of God's presence working through their humble lives. They kept no records.

In the union of Christ (lamp stand), the Holy Spirit (the oil), and the priesthood (the wicks), it was the oil that constantly needed to *be replenished* and the wicks that needed to *be trimmed* every morning and *lit* every evening.

We need to daily ask for a fresh supply of the Holy Spirit. When Paul writes to the Ephesians in 5:18, "Be filled with the Spirit," in the Greek it means, "Keep on being refilled."

If the light went out it, was because the priest *failed to put oil in* the lamps or he had not trimmed the wicks. It then no longer mattered that the lampstand was made of pure gold or that the oil was pure from beaten olives or that the fire that lit the lamps was from the altar.

When the *oil supply burns up*, the light goes out. When the *wick is not trimmed*, the oil flow and light is diminished. These *wicks* were made of the used linen robes of the priests. They were the greatest source of trouble because the fire would char the wick and then it would no longer draw the oil up to fuel the flame.

Devotions are a good way of trimming our wicks and

replenishing the oil. Since "the spirits of prophet are subject to prophets," (I Cor. 14:32) devotions are a good way to bring our minds into agreement with the spirit of prophecy. "Let the word of Christ richly dwell within you" (Col. 3:16), says Paul to the Colossians and to us, who as the believer priest is be a participant in the ministry of the holy place, not just an observer. "How blessed are those who observe His testimonies, who seek Him with all their heart" (Ps. 119:2).

Only when the believer priest is trimmed does he convey adequate oil for a bright light. If pride elevates the wick too high, there is too much smoke. If self depreciation keeps the wick too low, it will extinguish the flame or burn poorly for lack of oil.

Those *whose fires burn must have their wicks trimmed.* The portion that God trims from our life is the portion He has just finished using. Our testimonies need to be up to date and current as evidence that the wicks are trimmed and the oil is flowing and the flame is bright.

Where I live there are many hundreds of acres of raspberry bushes. These are trimmed every winter so it appears that only the bare main stems are left. One wonders how it will ever bare fruit again. A vineyard is also trimmed because the branch bearing fruit last year will not bear fruit again. So it is trimmed to make way for new growth. The very things we take pride in and want to preserve, God removes. Human expediency has never proven to be a good asset to spiritual progress.

As Moses lighted the lamps before the Lord with fire from the altar, and Aaron and his sons kept it in order continually, so has Jesus as our high priest also been entrusted with the work of keeping the light of the church trimmed, in order to be able to "present to Himself the church in all her glory, having no spot or wrinkle or any such thing. (Eph. 5:27).

When you feel like you are getting crushed, take notice of

what proceeds from your mouth. Is it a testimony of recognized grace and gratitude or murmuring and grumbling?

If God has to put us in a press to squeeze some concession from us, it is not fit to be used for the light that lights up the holy place and reveal the glories of our Redeemer.

Gold Covered Altar of Incense

Ex. 30:1–10

I in Them and You in Me . . . Perfected in Unity"

We come now to the altar of incense, the smallest of the articles of furniture in the tabernacle, which was nearest the ark where the presence of God was enthroned on the mercy seat beneath the two cherubim. In Heb. 9:4, we find this altar of incense in the same Holy of Holies as the ark.

During the annual Day of Atonement, three times the high priest entered into this holy of holies. First he brought incense. The rest of the year it burned only on the altar of incense, but on this day it also burned before the mercy seat (Lev. 16:12–13). Then he brought the blood of the bull of the sin offering for himself and sprinkled it on the east side of the mercy seat and on the floor before it. The third time the blood of the goat for the sin offering for the people was brought in and likewise applied, but was now also applied to the vessels in the holy place including the altar of incense.

All this to say there was a close connection between the ark and this altar of incense. Not surprising, since it typifies of *the intercession of the perfect life before the Father*, who was raised from the dead and received up into glory. "If then you have been raised with Christ, keep seeking the things above, where Christ is seated at the right hand of God" (Col. 3:1–4).

The acacia wood it was made of and overlaid with pure gold tells again of the incorruptible human nature of Jesus, overlaid with the deity of God.

The altar was 1 cubit square, and 2 cubits high (about ½ by1 meter). Its horns were of one piece with it (Ex. 30:2). The 1 *cubit* points us to the oneness of heart, mind and intended purpose of intercessor and God. In Luke 22:32, the verb tense indicates Jesus prayed only once for Peter. His testimony in I Pet. 1:2–5 indicates that the oneness of Jesus and His Father had fulfilled the intended purpose of the prayer. Peter was kept by the power of God.

The altar height of 2 *cubits* may point to man's need to discern and pray for God's higher ways in heaven and on earth. "As the heavens are higher than the earth, so are My ways higher than your ways, and my thoughts than your thoughts" (Isa. 55:9).

In I Chron. 17:16, the prayer of David exemplifies this as he sits before the Lord and begins by saying, "Who am I, O Lord God, and what is my house." There follows a beautiful prayer of humility, acknowledgement and submission without pride, hypocrisy, legalism or boasting. Here was a man after the heart of God. Although David had established a new order of singers and musicians for praising God before the tent of meeting, (I Chron. 6:32; 16:37), he did not make his dancing before the ark in the robe of a priest a career or part of a new religion.

Nathan saying "no" to David's good idea and great longing in verse 1 to build a temple might have aroused his spiritual pride if it had been there. But without arguing, David prepares and gives all the instructions for this new temple to Solomon and says, "All this the Lord made me understand in writing by His hand upon me" (I Chron. 28:19).

David had the humility of a servant, living for the honor of God and Israel, who *understood the dimensions of the altar of incense and practiced life and prayer accordingly.*

Some say this altar speaks of praise and worship with music and thanksgiving, but Psalm 104 says that we "enter His gates with thanksgiving and His courts with praise." That's in the outer court called the hieron. David knowing that, placed the musicians and singers east of the altar.

The controversy of song and music among God's people is longer than the history of the church. Even Jesus offered Israel something far better than the psalms of David in the hieron. He offered them Himself, the living water of the naos (John 7:38). Jesus did not deny Israel its song and music, but warned them that of everything carnal, not a stone would be left on top of another. God long ago, in His encounter with Lucifer was aware of music's potential for good or evil, and therefore set for it a boundary. Solomon followed David's instruction to place them east of the altar (II Chron. 5:12). I am saying the altar of incense is no place for controversy or personal preference.

What then do we do in the naos? Read David's prayer. It is full of servant talk, wanting to see the Master's will and purpose established for Israel and himself and God's honor for generations to come.

Nowhere do we see *the potential and cost of intercession* more graphically illustrated than in the garden of Gethsemane. The cost of "not my will, but Thy will be done" was huge. But so also was the effect and benefit.

To those who make the journey with Jesus from the gate to the altar of incense, Jesus says, "If you abide in Me and my words abide in you, ask whatever you wish, and it shall be done for you." This last phrase may be understood as, "I will speak it into existence for you."

This journey into the Father's presence is transforming. *It enlightens but also crucifies.* That's why Jesus said, "let him . . . take up his cross and follow me" (Matt. 16:24) There's a place for only one Master in the human heart. The cross will terminate any other master that competes for the throne.

The *foursquare* of this altar would point us again to the ends of the earth, indicating that intercession is for the remotest parts of the world. Paul, in I Tim. 2:1, urges "that entreaties and prayers, petitions and thanksgivings be made on behalf of all men." Intercession is a responsibility and privilege of the royal priesthood.

The *horns* speak of the power of God to effect change to the ends of the earth. The number of horns is not mentioned, and its absence may well testify that the intercession of Jesus is not just limited to the ends of the earth, but also affects the events in heaven.

As Jesus taught us to pray, "Your will be done on earth as it is done in heaven" (Matt. 6:10).

The Incense

Ex. 30:34

Maintains Complete Acceptance

The first thing God tells Moses about the altar of incense is its purpose. You shall make an altar as a place for burning incense (Ex. 30:1). God provided a place nearest His presence for intercession. There, the Jesus who loved me, sought me, bought me and ascended to the Father intercedes for me with the fragrance of His own perfections. There, "at the right hand of God" (Rom 8:34), He is "crowned with glory and honor" (Heb.2:7). For this reason was there a *crown of gold* around the top of the altar.

Jesus is not there interceding to complete a believer's justification, but to *maintain us* in the place of complete acceptance. "He is able to save forever those who draw near to God through Him" (Heb. 7:25) "There is no other name under heaven given among men by which we must be saved" (Acts 4:12).

Korah thought he could challenge that. In Numbers. 16 he is claiming equal nearness to God as Aaron. Since Korah was not chosen as a type of the great high priest who was to come, he became a vessel chosen by God to demonstrate His displeasure. All those connected with the rejection of God's chosen high priest were buried alive.

The following day (Num. 16:41), Israel's grumbling continues and God sends a plague among the Israelites. The plague was stopped when *Aaron takes incense among the living and the dead* (Num. 16:48). This was a foreshadowing of how Jesus would mediate and intercede on behalf of His people.

Those who want to be their own high priest like Korah will

perish like him and 15,000 others. I John 2:1 says "we have an advocate with the Father; Jesus Christ the righteous."

No one but the priests were allowed to handle the incense. King Uzziah tried and died an early death like Korah.

The *fire for burning the incense* came from the altar of sacrifice (Lev. 16:12; Num. 16:46) where the sin offering had been consumed. The work of intersession is based on the work of redemption.

> "Our High Priest pleads for no blessing which His blood has not purchased, and asks only for Divine justice for the sin that He has atoned. The blessing for which He pleads is according to God's estimate of the life which He gave. 'I have glorified Thee on the earth, having accomplished the work which Thou hast given Me to do' (John17:4). That was the foundation on which all His pleas were based and urged."

So writes A.W. Pink in his book gleanings in Exodus.

The trimming and lighting of the lamps morning and evening was always done together with the burning of incense. *The ministry of the light of the world is very much the result of the ministry of intercession.*

Jesus presented His own perfections to the Father as the basis for His requests. In contrast, our prayers are so faulty, we do not know how to pray as we should, our worship is so far below what ought to be that we need to approach the Father on the merits of Christ's life alone.

The prophet Micah understood this when he says, "I will bear the indignation of the Lord because I have sinned against Him, *until He pleads my case* and *executes justice for me.* He will bring me out to the light, and I will see His righteousness" (Micah 7:9).

Job's testimony to Eliphaz long before Micah lived was, "Even now, behold, *my witness* is in heaven, and *my advocate* is on high (Job 16:19). His reply to Bildad was, "As for me, I know that *my Redeemer* lives, and at the last He will take His stand on the earth" (Job 19:25).

The burning of incense was perpetual (Ex. 30:8). As the fire on the altar was always burning and the fragrance of incense was always rising, so He ever lives to make intercession for us. And because He is, we, too, should pray without ceasing, that our prayers should be perfected in Him.

In Ex. 30:34–38, the ingredients of the incense are named as *frankincense, stacte, onycha, and galbanum.* There was to be an equal portion of each, prepared by a perfumer, salted, pure and holy, and not to be used or copied by anyone else in Israel.

Only Jesus was perfectly able to combine the claims of God and the needs of man. He was righteous without compromise toward God, yet exceedingly tender toward man. He was faithful in obedience to His Father, no matter how the audience responded or reacted, yet He was full of compassion for sinners. He denounced error and human tradition, yet was patiently tender toward the ignorant. He possessed all the dignity and majesty of God, and yet was meek and lowly as incarnate man. No one ever had such perfectly equal portions of character.

That is why the *incense was fragrant* (Ex. 30:7). It testifies of the acceptability of Christ's intercession before the Father.

The *incense was also pure* (Ex. 30:35). Nothing of the carnal human flesh can contribute to the work of our Redeemer's intercession. Without Jesus as intercessor, there is no access to the Father.

The *incense was most holy* (Ex. 30:36). The work of Jesus in heaven is in keeping with everything that is in humble obedience.

The burning coal which had consumed the sacrifice and then consumed the incense was next taken to Isaiah to consume his iniquity. The, "woe is me," was now changed to, "Here am I. Send me" (Isa. 6:5–8).

Laborers in the Vineyard

Matt. 20

Working for a Wise Master

In Matt. 19:27, a man named Peter asks a question. "Behold we have left everything, what then will there be for us?" Or as we would say it now, "What will we get out of this?" Peter was responding to what he had just seen. A rich young ruler had walked away from Jesus, sad and grieved by the answer he had just received. In contrast to this, Peter thought he had done quite well. He had left his father's house, boat and fishing nets.

Jesus now teaches four lessons to correct some wrong thinking

Know your master

He assures all the disciples that they will sit on thrones judging the twelve tribes of Israel. He expands His answer to include all those who believe and have left fathers and mothers and brothers and sisters and houses for His sake. They shall receive many times as much and inherit the eternal life. Then He gives the warning.

> "But many who are first will be last and the last first–
> Matt.19:30.

> For the kingdom of heaven is like a land owner"–
> Matt.20:1

Chapter 20 is still the same topic. It is a parable to illustrate the "but" of Matt. 19:30 and answers Peter's question of, *"What then will there be for us?"* It illustrates the kingdom of heaven enlisting laborers who for various reasons agree to work in its vineyard. The disciples were among those hired as laborers. The rich young man also was invited, but found the requirement too hard and the pay too low. Jesus has taken this occasion to expose a problem in Peter's thinking about his master and to illustrate a remedy.

Trust your master

There are two kinds of laborers. Those *who agree* on the price of a day's wage (Matt. 20:2)–these know what they will receive at the day's end and are so reminded at that time. And then those who were hired on the 3rd, 6th, 9th, and 11th hour. These are all simply told, *"Whatever is right, I will pay you."* These will have to trust the landlord is fair. Everyone who will come to Jesus as the owner and Lord of His kingdom becomes a laborer in it.

It is true some come early in life and some come in the last hour of life, but we don't work to earn our salvation, nor do we work to bargain for what we think we deserve. That's the issue Jesus is addressing in response to Peter's question. Peter thought that because he had left everything, he now deserved more than the rich young ruler. This kind of thinking does not understand grace. It thinks there is merit in human goodness and that mercy is deserved. It was Jesus who had chosen Peter.

Neither he nor any other person would ever choose to follow Jesus had it not been for God's grace and mercy extended to them. Having responded to the call of God, we all become laborers and make a choice between bargaining for what we think we deserve or trusting the Master to give out of the abundance of His riches and pleasure.

Watch your master

There is another warning. The disciples had all watched the young ruler go away grieved and sad. They heard the response of Jesus to this departure and questioned, "Who then can be saved?" They, the poor, were comparing themselves to the blessed young ruler. Jesus was teaching them to *get their eyes off man and on to the grace of God* "with whom all things are possible" (Matt. 19:26). The rich young ruler may have become a laborer in God's vineyard a month or two or a year or two later. He may have become the great apostle Paul. We don't know. But from the parable, we do know that Jesus is clear about the consequences of those who watch their fellow workers instead of keeping their eyes on the master who hired them. The first shall be last. They get what they bargained for.

If we bargain for a day's wage, He may give it. If we bargain for popularity, he may give it. In the parable He gave them exactly what they bargained for, but those who trusted the master all received more than expected. Those who trust find that the master is "able to do exceeding abundantly beyond all that we ask or think, according to the power that works within us" (Eph 3:20).

Those who bargain with God will watch their fellow workers thinking they have preeminence among others. This has its roots in pride, not grace or mercy. When those who had been hired first came to receive their wages, they thought they would receive more (Matt. 20:10), because they had noticed that the others had not worked all the day in the heat.

Watching others in a spirit of pride is horribly destructive. It hinders every prayer we offer up to God, and destroys every relationship we could have enjoyed on earth. How blessed it is to have the grace and mercy of God flow through our lives into the hearts of others without being conscious of it.

Imitate your master

This introduces the third lesson for all disciples. The apostle Paul describes and illustrates this humility very succinctly for the Philippian church and us. "With humility of mind, let each of you *regard one another as more important than himself*" (Phil. 2:3). "And being found in the appearance of man, He humbled Himself . . . to the point of death, even death on a cross. Therefore also God highly exalted Him and bestowed on Him the name which is above every name, that at the name of Jesus, every knee should bow" (Phil. 2:8–10). Jesus had demonstrated that "The last shall be first" (Matt. 20:16).

The Character of Intercessors

Dan. 9

O Daniel, Man Of High Esteem

The parable recorded in Matt. 20 is only weeks before the high priestly prayer of Jesus recorded in John 17. Even though prayer in Matt. 20 is not the subject, it was important for those who were to lead in establishing the church that they learn what characterizes the kind of prayer Jesus himself offers up to the Father in John 17.

A number of other prayers are recorded by people like Moses in Ex. 32, David in I Chron. 17, Isaiah in 13:15, and Jeremiah in Lam. 3:55. We can find them in Ezra 9, Nehemiah 9, Daniel 9 and Paul records them in Eph.1, and C01.1. It should not be too surprising to find common characteristics among them. I have chosen the prayer of Daniel to illustrate the lessons presented to the disciples in Matt.20 were well established in the life of people like Daniel.

Here is a man continually on his knees three times a day, praying and giving thanks to God, though it lands him in the Lions' den. King Darius is impressed by Daniel, as servant of his God. He issues a decree that all men are to fear and tremble before the God of Daniel. "For He is the living God and enduring forever, And His Kingdom is one which will not be destroyed, And His dominion will be forever" (Dan. 6:26).

From the testimony of Darius the King, it is fair to say Daniel was a man who knew his God and lived a life that presented that knowledge to those who encountered him. *His intercession* was not deterred by threats against his life. *His visions* and encounters with angels blessed him and every generation to this present day.

His humility was not affected or diminished by these encounters. He did not think he was above others. He was just a laborer in God's kingdom in Babylon as Jeremiah was in Jerusalem. The prophesy of Jeremiah was to him the same truth as if an angel from heaven had spoken it.

When Daniel understands that 67 of the 70 years of exile are over, he gives his attention to the Lord God to seek Him by prayer and supplication with fasting, sackcloth and ashes.

Remember that the kind of revelations that Daniel received could easily have puffed up his pride. He was human like Paul, who in II Cor. 12:7 writes that "because of the surpassing greatness of the revelations, for this reason, to keep me from exalting myself, there was given me a thorn in the flesh a messenger from Satan, to buffet me, to keep me from exalting myself." Here were men whose lives and prayers were like the frankincense and three spices added in equal portions, rising before God as a fragrant aroma.

From Daniel's prayer in chapter 9, we can read that:

Daniel knows his God.

He knows God's word to Jeremiah (verse 2), that God is "great and awesome who keeps His covenant and mercy . . . (verse 4), to the Lord our God belongs mercy and forgiveness . . . (verse 9), He confirmed His word which He spoke against us . . . (verse 12), we have not made our prayer before the Lord our God . . . (verse 13), the Lord has kept the disaster in mind . . . God is righteous in all His works which He does . . . (verse 14), who brought Your people out of the land of Egypt . . . and made Yourself a name" (verse 15 NKJV). When our life and testimony are in agreement with the things we know of God, and know Him to be and to have done, then our prayers ascend like Frankincense before God.

Daniel acknowledges his need.

"I set my face toward the Lord God to make request by prayer ..."(verse 3). He associates himself some 30 times with the sins of his people. "We have sinned and committed iniquity (verse 5). We have not heeded Your servants the prophets (verse 6), all Israel has transgressed Your law ..."(verse 11 NKJV) A broken spirit before God acknowledges the need for grace and mercy. Bargaining with God over the merits of our virtues is not part of intercession.

Daniel appeals to the character of God.

"O Lord great and awesome God, who keeps His covenant and mercy ... (verse 4), to the Lord our God belongs mercy and forgiveness ... (verse 9), God is righteous in all the works which He does ... (verse 14), who brought Your people out of Egypt with a mighty hand and have made Yourself a great name ... (verse 15). O Lord according to all Your righteousness, I pray let Your anger and Your fury be turned away from Your city Jerusalem, Your Holy Mountain;" (verse 16 NKJV).

There is a depth of knowledge in the heart of Daniel that understands the heart of God. Daniel is not watching his fellow Jews. He is not waiting to see if anyone will start a prayer meeting. He is not comparing himself to others to see if they deserve what God gives them. He knows from the promises of God what lies in the heart of God and appeals to that.

Daniel understands he has no merit.

"Hear the prayer of Your servant and his supplications, and for the Lord's sake cause Your face to shine on your sanctuary (verse 17). Oh my God, incline Your ear and hear; open your eyes and see our desolations ... for we do not present our supplications ...

because of our righteous deeds but because of Your great mercies. Oh Lord, hear! Oh Lord. Forgive! Oh Lord, listen and act. Do not delay for Your own sake, my God," (verse 18–19 NKJV).

He is praying for the unconscious out flowing of God's provisions, signs and wonders so they could again live where His presence had been among them in Jerusalem. He was not asking for life to be made easier, or to see signs and wonders which would not be comprehended. He was asking for the lasting aroma of humility to overcome the stench of human pride.

Frankincense and the Three Spices

Ex. 30:34–38

Ingredients of Intercession

Faith, humility, forgiveness of sin, the evil one, these were things that drove Jesus to His Father in prayer. Pride, hypocrisy, legalism, ignorance, greed, iniquity, were things Jesus addressed in His ministry. People focused on problems such as poverty, illness, political oppression. Satan offers such things as miracles, mysteries and authority.

Here at the altar, God required four ingredients in equal proportions that expressed what made Jesus the beloved son of His Father such a sweet smelling aroma. It was the Father who required these four ingredients, "and that you shall beat some of it very fine" (Ex. 30:36). This beating is not unlike the mercy seat and lamp stand which were a hammered work.

And it was salted, meaning it was inviolably sure. It symbolized the unbending and complete self surrender of Jesus to the Father, with all impurity and hypocrisy being rejected.

Perhaps for the same reason there are four Gospel accounts presenting four portraits of Jesus as King, Servant, Man, and God, so there are four ingredients in the incense to describe His intercession.

From the prayers recorded in scripture, it is not difficult to find four common characteristics of intercession that would correspond with the four ingredients. They are mentioned on the previous pages in the prayer of Daniel and illustrated in the parable of Matt. 20. 1) They know their God—His promises and covenant. 2) They acknowledge their need—they don't bargain with

God. 3) They appeal to the character of God–they don't watch their fellow workers 4) In their humility they understand they have no merit–the first shall be last, and the last first.

Let's compare the four characteristics to four components of incense:

Frankincense in Hebrew is "lebonah" and means to be white. It is a gum resin with a balsamic odor, of the olibanum tree. It was to be pure.

The Hebrew for *pure* is "tahor," which indicates *a purity practically developed* and manifested. *Pure* as in gold in Hebrew is "zachar," and refers to its intrinsic nature.

In the incarnate nature of Jesus, there was no sin. He was "zachar." But in His office as Redeemer, He is spoken of as "tahor," "being made perfect" (Heb. 2:10), "and having been made perfect" (Heb. 5:9), "and made perfect forever" (Heb. 7:28). It speaks of perfecting the author of salvation through suffering. "Although He was a Son, He learned obedience from the things He suffered" (Heb. 5:8). This obedience to the heart and will of His Father was the pleasing aroma, the frankincense of His life that ascended up.

In the meal offering, frankincense was added to the handful of fine flour and burned in the fire, illustrating that the aroma of Jesus' life expressed complete acceptance of His consecration *to meet the needs of fallen man*. It was also placed on the bread in the holy place. Here again it expresses the aroma of His life as He presents Himself *on behalf of redeemed man* as a memorial before the Father. While at the Altar of Incense, the aroma of Jesus intercedes to *maintain redeemed man* in the presence of the Father.

It was this abiding in and knowing of the Father's heart that made Him the fragrant aroma. This is also true of those who abide in Jesus.

Stacte in Hebrew means "a drop." This is a powder obtained from the hardened drops of a fragrant gum resin found in the bark of the Myrrh bush. The *hardened drops had to be broken and crushed*. These drops, like each of the four ingredients, were crushed and pounded separately in a mortar and made very fine. Stacte was a very valuable spice.

In Jesus, there was no hardness of heart as with us, yet He was made sin on our behalf (II Cor. 5:21). He understands brokenness as no one else on earth, and He can plead on the merits of his own perfections for the hardness of our hearts.

A heart broken and crushed by suffering is a valuable gift and aroma before God. "I am like a broken vessel" (Ps. 31:12). "The Lord is near to the broken hearted and saves those who are crushed in Spirit" (Ps. 34:18). "The sacrifices of God are a broken spirit" (Ps. 51:17).

Onycha in Hebrew means *aromatic shell*, a shell of the perfumed mollusk. The better ones are found in *the deeper parts* of the Red Sea. The onycha powder is made from the horny lids of these Red Sea shells. It is prepared by grinding these, and then when roasting or burning the powder, it releases the oil on which its aromatic properties depend.

Here is an aroma that comes from *the deep*. "How great are Thy works, Oh God. Thy thoughts are very deep" (Ps. 92:5). Prayers of intercessors were cries and appeals from deep within their hearts. They were not comparing themselves to others. Since they knew the heart of God and were broken of self, will and ego, they appealed to the character of God.

Galbanum or chelbenah in Hebrew means *an odorous gum*. It exudes from the lower part of a ferula plant found at the Mediterranean Sea. It had a pungent smell and *preserved the scent* over a long period of time.

The love of humility has had such a lasting effect over the centuries. Paul describes this humility well in Phil. 2. It takes the place of a servant, it is willing to be last, it is everlasting and practiced long after the remembrance of signs and wonders are forgotten, it can see past the presence of sin to a heart that needs to be redeemed, and it enables us to see the grace that makes the power and glory of God approachable.

The Ark of the Covenant

Ex. 25:1016

The Half Has Not Been Understood

Ex. 25 is the first of about fifty chapters of instructions concerning the tabernacle. Here the ark, His dwelling place on earth, was first described. It appears that a temporary ark was first made by Moses himself (Deut. 10:1–5). In the ark of Ex. 25 were placed the two stone tablets of the law, Aaron's rod with bud, flower and fruit, and the golden jar of manna. The words of Jesus in Ps. 40:8 "Thy law is within my heart" would indicate how closely His law and mercy seat and throne were tied together in His heart.

It is significant that two things of Jesus are quite consistently mentioned in the same order. Paul writes for example, " . . . that I may know Him," which speaks of *His person–who he is–*"and the power of His resurrection," which speaks of *what He has done* (Phil. 3:10).

We mostly emphasize first what He has done. The scriptures emphasize first who He is. The High priest first brought in his handful of incense, as a type of the fragrant perfections of Christ, *the person.* Then he brought in the blood of the sin offering illustrating *His work* of redemption (Lev. 16:12,14). John the Baptist first called Him "the Lamb of God"–*who He is.* Then he said, "Who takes away the sin of the world"–*what He did* (John 1:29). John writes, "I saw between the throne . . . and the elders a lamb standing,"–*who He is–*"as if slain"–*what He did* (Rev. 5:6). "Thus it was in this order of the Tabernacle furniture: first the ark, which tells of Christ the Person, then the mercy seat, etc., which point to His work," writes A. W. Pink in *Gleanings in Exodus.*

The ark itself was a chest made of the Acacia tree, found in the arid Sinai desert and around the Dead Sea. It grows in very dry soil to a maximum height of about 5 meters, provides *very hard durable insect resistant wood,* and has very long, sharp thorns. Piercing the bark at nightfall causes the "gum-arabic" to ooze out. This gum is useful for medicines and commerce. Though now crowned with glory and honor, Jesus was crowned on earth with thorns and was pierced in the darkness, causing blood to flow from His side for the healing of sin sick man.

The wood speaks of His human nature, which gave *form and dimension* to the ark. The gold, which covered it, speaks of His divine nature, which gave the ark its *appearance of glory and beauty.* In this we see again that His divine nature was displayed over the form of a servant.

The dimensions were 2½ cubits long, 1½ cubits wide, and 1½ cubits high. The ½ cubit would indicate we can only comprehend a part of the glories of Christ. Even in His flesh, He did not fully reveal Himself. If He had, all Israel would have been blinded like Saul on the road to Damascus (Acts 9:8), and they would have shared in the same fear as the disciples at the transfiguration of Jesus on the Mountain (Mark 9:2–8).

The equal dimensions for height and width would indicate the *equal satisfaction* He brought to the needs of His Father for holy perfection and the needs of sinful man for a redeemer to restore them to original condition.

Heb. 9:4 mentions three items in the ark.

The moral law written on two tables of stone was placed in the ark. In Ex. 37:1, Bezalel made the ark. In Deut. 10:1–4 it says Moses made the ark. It appears that Moses made a temporary chest for the law until the golden ark was made. The first tables Moses threw to the ground, and they were broken, pointing to the law the first Adam had broken. The second writing of the law was placed in this ark of wood without gold. This time the law is kept by the perfect man, Jesus–the second Adam. In His humiliation, He magnified the law and made it honorable. The gold-covered ark of Bezalel speaks of this second Adam as now glorified. The mention of only the law in the ark in I Kings 8:9 is in context of the temple dedication, which pointed to the coming Kingdom and the eternal law that shall rule it.

The jar of manna presents a similar issue. In Ex. 16:33 Moses tells Aaron to take a jar and put in an omer of manna and place it before the Lord. This was before the tabernacle was built. This common jar points to Israel expecting a Messiah that was to be a physical descendant of Abraham and David. When He came, He presented Himself as the Son of God, born of the Spirit, and we now know Him to be crowned with glory and honor, pointing to the gold jar. In Heb. 9:4 it is a golden jar holding manna in the ark, and all three items mentioned point to God's provisions in Christ while they were on their journey through the wilderness. The manna foreshadowed Christ as providing and being the food of His pilgrim people. It was God's provision of "grace." John speaks of this Jesus as, "full of grace and truth" (John 1:14).

The budded rod story is in Num. 17. The issue was Aaron's priestly authority. So the tribal rods as symbols of authority were laid before God to be decided by Him. The dead rod of Aaron appears next morning with bud, flower and fruit. Where Moses as prophet proclaimed truth, Aaron as priest expressed grace. Both were hated without cause. Jesus, also full of grace and truth, was despised and rejected and killed. But like the dead rod of Aaron, He came to life again. This rod of "grace" was to be put before/in the ark as a witness against the rebels "that you may put to an end their grumbling against me so that they should not die" (Num. 17:10). This was the priestly ministry of Aaron–*to preserve God's people before Him.*

The pot of manna was a bread from heaven to *strengthen Israel*. The rod of Aaron was a symbol of priestly grace to *sustain Israel*. The two tables of stone inscribed by the finger of God's glory with the terms of the covenant were to *humble Israel*.

The Mercy Seat

Ex. 25:17–22

There I Will Meet With You

Here is where God established His presence on earth. The mercy seat typified the divine throne of God. It was a place of judgment transformed by the sprinkled blood into a place of mercy and throne of grace

It was the place where *mercy covered over the law* and the value of the propitiation of Jesus witnessed before God. This witness was based on the altar of sacrifice as the place where propitiation was made.

God was appeased. He was satisfied with Jesus through whom His judgments against the sins of His people were removed. In Him the requirements of the law and all the attributes of God were satisfied.

Propitiation is the act by which *Jesus gained our forgiveness and God's favor.* "And He Himself is the propitiation for our sins and not only ours, but also for those of the whole world" (I John 2:2). "In this is love, not that we loved God, but that He loved us and sent His Son to be the propitiation for our sins" (I John 4:10).

At the annual day of atonement in Lev. 16:14, Aaron takes the blood of the bullock offered on the altar, and with his finger sprinkled it on the east side of the mercy seat. This was nearest the veil and the direction of approach. This proclaimed that God had *accepted the victim* offered to Him and the way of approach was now open.

Next, Aaron was to sprinkle some of the blood seven times on the ground in front of the mercy seat (Lev. 16:14). This testified of the *perfection of our standing* before Him with no more fear of judgment or condemnation.

While there was the *mercy seat* for God, there was no chair for the priests because their work was never finished and needed constant repetition. God found His rest on the perfect and finished work of His Son.

> "And there I will meet with you from above the mercy seat, between the cherubim."–Ex. 25:22

> "The Lord reigns, let the earth tremble, He sits between the cherubim, let the earth be moved."–Ps. 99:1.

God's satisfaction in Christ is easily forgotten by our hardened hearts of unbelief and our emphasis on feelings. Our culture is indoctrinated to think with its feelings and listen with its eyes. But God says we need to be transformed by the renewing of our minds.

It is true that Jesus died in the place of His people, but also on behalf of God. *God's law had to be kept and vindicated. His justice needed to be satisfied.* Mercy could not be given to man at the expense of justice.

"Righteousness and justice are the foundation of Your throne" (Ps 89:14).

The dimensions of the mercy seat were the same as the ark. The crown around the top of the ark kept the mercy seat in its place. The thickness of the lid is not mentioned nor is it stated how much gold was used for the lid and the two cherubim. Perhaps it is omitted to indicate that "as the heavens are high above the earth, so great is His mercy toward them that fear Him" (Ps. 103.11). It is stated that it was made as a hammered work (Ex. 37:7). Just like the lamp stand. Many were the strokes and blows that hit Him.

That the width and length were the same as the ark would

indicate that though His mercy is great, *it does not extend past the finished work of Christ* to fulfill the law and is applied only to those who stand on the sprinkled blood of Jesus before God.

God's grace reigns "through righteousness to eternal life through Jesus Christ our Lord" (Rom. 5:21).

Cherubim were on both ends of the Mercy Seat. These beings are associated with the administration of God's judicial authority. Such as the cherubim at the east entrance of the Garden of Eden.

On the mercy seat their heads are bowed down. Here, as the administrators of God's judicial authority, they are witness to God's plan of redemption for His people.

Though the cherubim had the knowledge of the law, here it was hid from there view. God covered it over with the mercy seat. So they only saw the blood of the life it represented between the law and its keeper. At the appointed hour of judgment, they will know how to apply their judicial authority, having witnessed the blood-stained mercy seat. Angels must wait a little longer to understand. "The sufferings of Christ and His glories which were to follow, are things which angels desire to look into" (I Pet. 1:11–12).

Without the mercy seat, the law could only condemn. The only person who then could stand before God would be the Son of Man. He could then have condemned the entire human race, but He didn't.

The heart which kept the law unbroken received the penalty of those who deserved it. Without the mercy seat, the ark is but a place of judgment.

The people of Beth Shemesh found this out when they lifted the mercy seat and looked into the ark. More than 50,000 people died.

"No one comes to the Father but though me" (John 14:6). By faith in the only one who fulfilled the law. *He was as pure as the mercy seat was "pure gold"* (Ex. 25:17).

From that place of pure perfection, God said, "There I will meet with you; from above the mercy seat, from between the cherubim, which are upon the ark of the testimony" (Ex. 25:22).

Sin no longer needs to stand between us. "Therefore brethren, having boldness to enter the Holiest by the blood of Jesus, by a new and living way which He consecrated for us through the veil, that is, His flesh ... let us draw near with a sincere heart ..." (Heb. 10:19–22).

The Ark

Num. 4

Its coverings, its names, its travels

The structure of the tabernacle was made to be mobile and transported on ox carts. Its furniture components were to be carried by the priesthood. Its travels were extensive. For forty years the ark journeyed from resting place to resting place in the wilderness. Each time the encampment was to move, the priesthood was to first cover the furniture, beginning with the ark.

This dwelling place of God was first covered with the *veil* that separated the two tabernacle compartments. Here was the deity of Jesus (the ark) covered in His humanity (the veil), while He traveled His wilderness journey here on earth for thirty three years. This was covered with *badger skins*, telling us it was not His outward appearance that attracted people to Him. There was a third cover over the ark that was *pure blue*. This was the only vessel with this as its outer layer, testifying of its heavenly origin.

While we are on this subject of coverings, we may as well mention what covered the other vessels of the tabernacle.

On the table of bread, the lampstand and the altar of incense, this *blue* cover was the first layer to cover them. The table was then covered with a cloth of *scarlet red*. This table is in remembrance of the resurrected Jesus who took His own blood into the heavenly tabernacle on our behalf to the Father's delight.

The altar of sacrifice had a *purple* cloth as a first layer. Purple is the combination of blue and red. This tells of the glorious perfections of deity, combined with the faultless life of obedience that Jesus brought as the perfect sacrifice of satisfaction for the sin of the world.

The covering of *badger skins* over these four items tells us again what God has always known. To carnal human flesh, these holy revelations of what God has done for us in Jesus Christ are of no interest or attraction.

What you may have noticed is that for the laver, neither the covering nor the means of transport is mentioned. It may be that since it was made of solid bronze, it would have been too heavy for the Levites to carry. I think there was another reason, also. Since it is in type Jesus, the Word of God, it is to be seen, examined, read, heard, held, owned and carried by all.

The ark is given seven descriptive titles.

It is first mentioned as *the ark of the testimony* (or of the law), from which God spoke and where the testimony of His law was kept. (Ex. 25:22).

Jesus not only fulfilled the law, He is the center of God's council. After the crossing of the Jordan River, it is no longer referred to by this term. Israel's acceptance of what God had spoken was laid as a testimony in the ark.

When Israel leaves Mount Horeb on a three-day journey, it is now spoken of as the *ark of the covenant of the Lord* journeying in front of them (Num. 10:33). Throughout the following years of grumbling and failure to trust God, He ever remained faithful and true to His covenant.

After the victory at Ai, Joshua builds an altar of uncut stones and carves a copy of the law on stones. He places half the people on the mount Gerizim side of the valley and the other half on Mount Ebal side of the valley. With this *ark of the covenant of the Lord* placed between them, he reads to this new generation of Israel, who only a few weeks before were marked with the covenant sign of circumcision, the terms of the covenant in all the words of the law, its blessing and curses. While we as God's people have always failed in keeping this covenant, "Jesus has become the guarantee of a better covenant" (Heb. 7:22). He fulfilled its responsibilities and obligations.

At the crossing of the Jordan, it is called *the ark of the covenant of the Lord of all the earth* (Josh. 3:11). The Lord of all the earth was laying claim to His land even though it had not been conquered yet.

While God did not attach His name to any of the other vessels of the tabernacle, He did do so with the ark. It was called the ark of the Lord, and *the ark of God* (I Sam. 3:3). The ark speaks more to the deity of Christ, of who Christ is, while the other vessels speak more of what He has done.

The term *the ark of the Lord God* comes from the Hebrew Adonai Jehovah. Adonai means headship, Lord, one who purposes to bless. And Jehovah means God, the self existent one, who is in covenant relationship. King Solomon uses this term when he addresses Abiathar the priest for having conspired to make Solomon's older brother king. Having carried the *ark of the Lord God* during David's reign, his life is spared, though he now deserved to die for violating the Lord God's revealed will (I Kings 2:26).

The ark is spoken of as *the holy ark* by king Josiah in II Chron. 35:3. Holiness is an expression of one's conduct and obedience to what God has said. His passion was to restore the ark to its proper place in the holy of holies. It seems it was again carried by the Levites, had been removed from its resting place and substituted by vessels made for Baal, Asherah, and the hosts of heaven (II Kings 23:4).

In the Psalms of Ascents, Psalm 132 expresses how David had sworn to the Lord and said, "I will not give sleep to my eyes, until I find . . . a dwelling place for the Mighty One of Jacob." He is referring to the ark, God's footstool and resting place on earth. He calls it "*the ark of Your strength.*" When this ark had been captured and set before the Philistine god Dagon, it fell on its face, broken before the ark.

When the strength and glory of God is set before us, will we see the idols of our worship fallen down and broken, or will we find Him to be the ark of our strength and resting place of our faith?

The tabernacle and its contents as well as the entire volume of history and testimony of God's people were recorded, preserved and compiled as the scriptures for instruction and encouragement so that we may "know."

The apostle John uses this word 27 times in his first letter and writes in verse 13 of the last chapter:

> "These things I have written to you who believe in the name of the Son of God, in order that you may know that you have eternal life."

The three dimensional imagery of the tabernacle has had a great deal to teach us about this knowing.

The apostle Paul, as he writes to the Philippian church about the surpassing value of knowing, also uses imagery in the third chapter. As an accountant who looks at his past, he says "I count." He writes as an athlete who looks at his present and says "I press on." And as an alien on this planet, he looks to the future and writes, "we wait."

In reminding them of the futility of his past accomplishments compared to knowing Christ he writes,

> "But whatever things were gain to me those things I have counted as loss for the sake of Christ. More than that, I count all things to be loss in view of the surpassing value of knowing Christ Jesus my Lord, for whom I have suffered the loss of all

things, and count them but rubbish in order that I may gain Christ, and may be found in Him not having a righteousness of my own, derived from the law, but that which is through faith in Christ, the righteousness which comes from God through faith, that I may know Him, and the power of his resurrection and the fellowship of His sufferings, being conformed to His death; In order that I may attain to the resurrection from the dead.–Phil. 3:7–11

In reminding them of his present circumstances, he writes not only of his dissatisfaction, but also of his devotion, his direction, his determination and discipline.

Not that I have already obtained it or have already become perfect, but I press on in order that I may lay hold of that for which also I was laid hold of by Christ Jesus. Brethren, I do not regard myself as having laid hold of it yet; but one thing I do: forgetting what lies behind and reaching forward to what lies ahead, I press on toward the goal for the prize of the upward call of God in Christ Jesus. Let us therefore, as many as are perfect, have this attitude; and if in anything you have a different attitude, God will reveal that also to you; however, let us keep living by that standard to which we have attained.–Phil. 3:12–16

In reminding them of the future, he warns of the enemies of the gospel but also writes of certain transformation to come.

Brethren, join in following my example, and observe those who walk according to the pattern you have in us. For many walk, of whom I often told you, and now tell you even weeping, that they are enemies of the cross of Christ, whose end is destruction, whose god is their appetite, and whose glory is in their shame, who set their minds on earthly things. For our citizenship is in heaven, from which also we eagerly wait for a savior, the Lord Jesus Christ; who will transform the body of our humble state into conformity with the body of His glory, by the exertion of the power that He has even to subject all things to Himself.–Phil. 3:17–21

The imagery and testimony of the tabernacle was and remains an illustration of this knowing of Christ and His transforming power.

Psalms of Ascent

Psalms 120–134

From Living among Gentiles to Resurrection Glory

The series of Psalms from 120–134 begins with life lived among the gentiles and terminates with a great doxology. Our journey through the tabernacle has followed this same order. Our comprehension of all that the tabernacle, its vessels and ark with its mercy seat represents of coming glory is only dimly understood. What we do understand is very helpful and encouraging to the faith given and entrusted to us. Not many in history past have had Paul's experience of a visit to the third heaven and then not being allowed to talk about it.

So it is not surprising that Psalm 134 is a rather brief conclusion to the Psalms of Ascent. But it is a doxology of how things will end. It is not unlike knowing something of what Jesus said in Matthew 24 and 25. These two chapters are also a very brief summary of events at the conclusion of history. Many of the details of the last days are missing, so we have some acquired information but not the entire picture. Even so, Jesus said "when you see all these things, recognize that He is near, right at the door." (Matt. 24:33). So there is enough information given in order to "know."

I have not found the life that is to be lived in the holy place to be something that just drops from heaven so I can just put it on like a garment. There are changes that need to take place inside, and these seem to come painfully and slow. Let me repeat here what I said at the end of my opening remarks of the first pages. It is helpful in the perfections of Christ to see what is missing in our own lives, what needs to be put on, why it is not working, what has been put on and what is overemphasized. In all of this, the humility of Jesus will be our greatest liberating friend and asset.

These Psalms of Ascent were Pilgrim songs sung by the people as they went up to Jerusalem for the annual feasts of Passover, Pentecost, and Tabernacles. God had instructed the construction of tabernacles and temple in accurate detail of the typology of the coming Redeemer and King. We should not be surprised to find, then, that He now also arranged an order of Psalms to be sung that correlates to the entire journey of man. It begins where he lives among people of unclean lips and lying tongues and progresses to the place where God lives in the holy of holies. The journey terminates there with a benediction and blessing from God. He was putting on the lips of Israel, in song and music, the fullness of their Redeemer. Much of Israel may have understood very little of it, as their idolatry would indicate. But the images of God's own testimony were being sung and passed on to the next generation as they went to the place of God's residence on earth. It is my view that Paul's instruction to the Colossian Christians to "Let the word of Christ dwell in you richly, in all wisdom, teaching and admonishing one another with psalms and hymns and spiritual songs, singing with grace in your hearts to the Lord" (Col. 3:16 NKJV), was not just a good idea he had. It was in keeping with God's intent that His bride the church needed to carry on this message in word and song. If the church was to be a tabernacle, it needed to know what the tabernacle looked like and its contents known and understood.

Now let me take you briefly through these Psalms and try to illustrate in their sequence and content how they follow the pattern of the tabernacle. Take particular notice of that in the opening verses of each of the Psalms.

Psalm 120 tells of his life among the gentiles:

He was living among a people of lying lips and deceitful tongues. He says, "I sojourn in Meshech" (verse 2), which was the name of a son of Japhet, which became the gentile nations. "I dwell among the tents of Kedar" (verse 3), which was the name of a son of Ishmael, from which the Arabs and Islam have descended.

I am for peace, but when I speak," they are for war (verse 7).

Psalm 121 deals with His reason for beginning his journey to Jerusalem.

He is on his way to Jerusalem and takes notice of what is on the hilltops.

"I will lift up my eyes to the mountains" (verse 1), where the places of idolatry and gentile worship were located (Eze.6:13, 20:28).

He then asks the question, "From whence shall my help come?" This begins a new sentence in the text, and is answered in verses 2–8. His help will not come from the idols on hilltops, but from the Lord who made everything. Who does not allow the feet of His people to slip, and as the keeper of Israel He does not slumber nor sleep. He stands by Israel day and night, protects them from all evil and keeps their soul while guarding their going out and coming in now and forever.

Psalm 122 tells of his arrival at the gates of Jerusalem.

When he arrives, he remembers with gladness the announcement of going to Jerusalem and the house of the Lord.

"Our feet are standing within your gates, O Jerusalem" (verse 2). It is the "Spirit of Wisdom" (Isa.11:2) that leads us to turn from unbelief, to leave the world's foolishness and enter through the gate of the temple for the purpose of giving thanks to the name of the Lord (verse 4).

He enters its gates because it is the place of the throne of the House of David from which He will rule the world. And he enters to pray for the peace of Jerusalem and commits himself to live and uphold the good name of God who lives there.

Psalm 123 finds him entering its courts with praise.

"Unto You I lift up my eyes, O You who dwell in the heavens" (verse 1).

Take notice now the form his praise takes in verse 2: " . . . as the eyes of servants look to the hand of their master, as the eyes of a maid looks to the hand of her mistress; So our eyes look to the Lord our God." Hand signals were a common form of directing servants to provide for their masters. Servants had to be very attentive not to miss the signals.

The humility of servitude that looks for instruction and direction is a necessary component of praise. The idea here is to come before God with a life that is attentive to mercy, truth, righteousness and justice. Amos makes this point in chapter 5:21–27. Music and song were not forbidden, but neither were they a substitute for these.

Praise acknowledges our need for God to "be gracious to us" as we have extended this grace to others. God loves those who acknowledge their need for Him. We confess our need even while " . . . we are greatly filled with contempt" (verse 3) not just for our own personal guilt but also the guilt and contempt of the proud who are at ease in their scoffing of God (verse 4).

Psalm 124 brings back the remembrance of his past redemption.

The "spirit of understanding" (Isa. 11:2) enables us at the altar of sacrifice to understand our redemption.

He begins by confessing that, "Had it not been the Lord who was on our side . . . then they would have swallowed us alive . . . Then the raging waters would have swept over our soul" (verses1,3,5).

The redeemed of God are "kept by the power of God" (I Pet. 1:5). They are secured by a blood covenant already promised to Adam and Eve, Noah, Abraham, Moses, and demonstrated at the Passover, the sacrifices, Calvary and the communion cup.

It is by this redemption that "our soul has escaped as a bird out of the snare of a trapper (verse 7). The snare of sin is broken, and we have escaped the judgment of condemnation.

"Our help (redemption) is in the name of the Lord (Jesus Christ) who made heaven and earth (verse 8). He it was who gave Himself up for us as an offering and sacrifice to God.

Psalm 125 is a testimony to his present security.

This security is for "those who trust in the Lord."

The Lord became not only our redeemer to secure our redemption, but also as "the Word became flesh and dwelt among us" (John 1:14) to sanctify us. It is the laver that pointed to Him as the Word and the "Spirit of Council" (Isa. 11:2). The laver washes us for sanctification "by the renewing of the mind" (Rom. 12:2). This makes God's people "as Mount Zion that cannot be moved, but abides forever" (verse 1). Because "you have been born again not of seed which is perishable, but imperishable, that is through the living and abiding word of God" (I Pet. 1:23).

"As the mountains surround Jerusalem, so the Lord surrounds His people" (verse 2). "and His name is called "The Word of God" (Rev. 19:13). This Word sanctifies, washes, councils, instructs, guides, protect, admonishes, and directs the people of God to know Him and walk in His ways and be "upright in their hearts" (verse 4).

Those who refuse the council of God will see their iniquity visited upon them and their children (verse 5).

Ps. 126 testifies of God's people delighting in His abiding presence.

"When the Lord brought back the captive ones of Zion, we were like those who dream. Then our mouth was filled with laughter and our tongue with joyful shouting; Then they said among the nations, The Lord has done great things for them. The Lord has done great things for us; We are glad" (verses 1–3).

Jesus, the bread of life, was presented on the table of bread as a memorial before the Father, representing His people in resurrection glory. It tells of the "Spirit of Strength" (Isa. 11:2) strengthening his people by the delight of His abiding presence in the Father and in us.

Isaiah prophesied of Him as "My Chosen one in Whom My Soul delights" (Isa.42:1). The Father said of Him, "You are my beloved Son, in You I am well pleased" (Luke 3:22). Jesus has done great things for us. He has delivered us from the captivity of sin and renewed our minds to think humility instead of pride. We have great reason to delight in Him, the bread of life. Even when faith fails us, He remains faithful.

What faith "sows in tears" we "shall reap with joyful shouting" (verse 5). Jesus wept over Jerusalem, carried His bag of seed and sowed this seed of faith to the ends of the earth, and it has reaped a bountiful harvest of redeemed people. It is solemn to remember Him broken to redeem us, but with delight and gladness we celebrate His provisions of resurrection glory for us.

Ps. 127 tells of a life under God's direction bearing much good fruit.

Here we see life lived in the light of the lampstand as the "Spirit of Knowledge" (Isa. 11:2) brings God's direction to man.

Three times, we are warned of the vanity of those who labor, watch and worry too many hours over house and food and clothes. Those who know the Lord can trust Him. They labor not for results, but for fruit. Our carnal, cultural, vision-oriented, goal setting, success-driven, user-friendly, seeker-sensitive and results-guided time allotments for getting things done have produced some very sour grapes.

Fruit is something that grows by abiding on a vine or on a branch. It takes time and nourishment to develop. God is looking for good fruit (Isa. 5:2). Jesus and His bride, the Church, are also meant to be fruitful and multiply. A growing church with a quiver full of the born again does not " . . . need to be ashamed when they speak with their enemies in the gate" (Ps.127:5). They are safe and secure, kept by the power of God.

The Spirit of God, knowing the heart of God, will bear the fruit that pleases God. "But we all with unveiled face, beholding as in a mirror the glory of the Lord are being transformed into the same image from glory to glory just as from the Lord the Spirit" (II Cor. 3:18). That's good fruit

Psalm 128 portrays the life of intercession bearing much fruit.

Isaiah prophesies of Jesus that "He will see His offspring, He will prolong His days, and the good pleasure of the Lord will prosper in His hand. As a result of the anguish of His soul He will see it and be satisfied" (Isa. 53:10).

It was the sweet aroma that ascended from the altar of incense that bore witness of "the Spirit of the Fear of the Lord" (Isa.11:2) in the life of Jesus.

"How blessed is every one who fears the Lord, who walks in His ways. When you eat of the fruit of your hands you will be happy and it will be well with you" (Ps. 128:1,2). How true this is of intercession and the fruit of answered prayer.

Much of Israel's comprehension of God was through physical evidence of things like law, tabernacle, temple, psalms, kings, prophets, priests, land, prosperity and children. So when the psalms were sung by the men, women and children of Israel on their way to the temple, they were constant reminders to Israel of God's promises, warnings and expressions of Israel's relationship to their Redeemer. So it is not surprising then to read the psalmist say that to fear the Lord is to also eat the fruit of your hands, to be happy, to have a home with children like olive plants around the table (verses 2,3).

For the church Jesus modified this list somewhat. God would not just be among them and in His temple as He was for Israel, but He would be in them as the temple. They would be strangers and aliens, mocked and ridiculed, jailed and killed, humiliated and rejected. They would pray for those who persecuted them and bear much fruit. God has always been looking for good fruit (Isa. 5:2).

Jesus spoke the same message in John 15. "The branch cannot bear fruit unless it abides in the vine. He who abides in

Me and I in him, he bears much fruit." (verse 4,5). The fruit of labor, ministry and answered prayer (verse 7). "These things I have spoken to you, that My joy may be in you, and that your joy may be full" (verse 11). "You did not choose Me, but I chose you and appointed you that you should go and bear fruit, and that your fruit should remain. We see this applied in Psalm 128:6 to their children's children or from generation to generation. Everyone who fears the Lord, who walks in His ways, will seek to avail themselves of the promise of the altar of incense, "that whatever you ask of the Father in My name, He may give you" (John 15:16).

The Lord bless you from Zion. The city of David, the home of the tabernacle of David, the temple of Solomon, but also the shadow image of the home of Jesus, our great intercessor before the throne of God.

Psalm 129 characterizes stacte as the first of three spices of the incense.

Stacte was from the hardened drops of the gum resin of the Myrrh bush. These drops had to be broken and crushed to a fine powder.

David foreshadowed the experience of Jesus when he said, "I am forgotten as a dead man, out of mind, I am like a broken vessel (Ps. 31:12). Yet he was comforted by the assurance that, "The Lord is near to the brokenhearted, and saves those who are crushed in spirit (Ps. 34:18).

David could testify that, "Many times they have persecuted me from my youth up; Yet they have not prevailed against me. The plowers plowed upon my back. They lengthened their furrows" (Ps. 129:2,3). Jesus knows about this. "All discipline for the moment seems not to be joyful, but sorrowful, yet to those who have been trained by it, afterwards it yields the peaceable fruit of righteousness" (Heb. 12:11).

The destiny of those who hate Zion and inflict this grinding and persecution is that they cannot be taught or changed by the grace of suffering and persecution (verses 5–7).

These enemies of Zion know how to inflict pain, but cannot speak the blessing of God upon His people, for they are filled with pride (verse 8).

Psalm 130 characterizes onycha as the second spice added to the incense.

The psalmist is quite clear about the place he is in. "Out of the depths I have cried to thee Oh Lord" (verse1). Depth is important. Shallow soil does not sustain growth. Mark 4:5.

It is from the horny lid of a shell found in the deep parts of the red sea that onycha is made. "Oh the depth of the riches both of the wisdom and knowledge of God. How unsearchable are His judgments and unfathomable His ways" (Rom. 11:33). "He reveals the deep and secret things" (Dan 2:22). "For the Spirit searches all things, even the depths of God" (I Chron 2:10).

God searches us deeper than we do ourselves. When He shows us our iniquities, we ask, "Oh Lord, who could stand? But there is forgiveness with You, That You may be feared" (Ps. 130:3,4 NKJV).

This is the outcome of iniquities forgiven. To be enabled with depth of understanding to intercede with Godly compassion for others according to the Spirit of the Fear of the Lord. From the depths we can find ourselves in, it is important to trust and wait patiently. For with the Lord there is loving kindness and abundant redemption (verses 5–7).

The grace that has saved multitudes of Gentiles will also save Israel (verse 8).

Psalm 131 characterizes galbanum as the third spice in the incense.

When the prophet Nathan said to David he was not to build the temple, King David went in and sat before the Lord, and he said, "Who am I, O Lord God? And what is my house, that You have brought me this far?" (I Chron. 17:16 NKJV). David here is not unlike Moses, the most humble man on earth, who would go in and sit before the Lord. This humility is a necessary component for intercession.

David can truthfully say, "Oh Lord my heart is not proud, nor my eyes haughty. Nor do I involve myself in great matters, or in things too difficult for me" (Ps. 131:1). Haughtiness and ambition are two great obstacles to answered prayer.

Galbanum is a gum from the lower part of the ferula plant and points to this humility. Its odor is pungent and only pleasing when mixed with other spices. It gives them lasting effect.

When humility is added to the frankincense (the knowing of God, His promises and covenants and word), to stacte (the brokenness that comes from pain and suffering and rejection), and to onycha (a depth of reverence and awe for the holy perfections of God), then a pleasing aroma of intercession ascends to God and brings lasting effect and blessing to man.

In contrast to haughtiness and great ambition, David can say, "Surely I have composed and quieted my soul; Like a weaned child rests against his mother, my soul is like a weaned child within me" (Ps. 131:2). Jesus also testified of the need for humility to His disciples by putting a child before them and saying, "Whoever then humbles himself as this child, he is the greatest in the Kingdom of heaven" (Matt. 18:4).

Psalm 132 presents us an illustration of David's intercession.

Somewhere during or shortly after the time David had constructed his own palace, he reminds God of having made a vow in time past. "How he swore to the Lord, and vowed to the Mighty One of Jacob, 'Surely I will not enter my house, nor lie on my bed; I will not give sleep to my eyes, or slumber to my eyelids; Until I find a place for the Lord, a dwelling place for the Mighty One of Jacob" (Ps. 132:2–5). That is strong language.

His prayer now seems to move to the arks' present location in the field of Jaar (Kirjath Jaerim) 8 miles to the north "Let us go in to His dwelling place. Let us worship at His footstool (verses 6,7). It then reads like he is praying for the ark to be moved from there to the temporary place he had prepared for it in Jerusalem. "Arise O Lord to Your resting place; You and the ark of Your strength" (verse 8 NKJV).

His closing request is not just for himself. "For the sake of David Your servant, do not turn away the face of Your anointed" (verse10 NKJV). This would also refer to each successive Davidic King until the Messiah takes His place on the throne.

How wonderfully comprehensive, simple and brief is David's prayer. He remembers his past vow. He is presently seeking to fulfill it. He asks for future generations to inherit his anointing.

God's answer in verses 13–18 seems to be equally brief and comprehensive.

"For the Lord has chosen Zion; He has desired it for His habitation. This is my resting place forever; Here I will dwell . . . I will abundantly bless her provision . . . Her priests I will clothe with salvation; and her godly ones will sing aloud for joy. There I will cause the horn of David to spring forth . . . His enemies I will clothe with shame; But upon Himself his crown shall shine."

How fitting are the words of Jesus in John 15:7. "If you abide in me and my words abide in you, ask whatever you wish and it shall be done for you."

Psalm 133 brings us to the dwelling place of the presence of God

Here on the mercy seat of the Ark of the Covenant God himself as the 'Spirit of the Lord" (Isa. 11:2) said He would meet with His people.

"Behold how good and how pleasant it is, for brothers to dwell together in unity" (Ps. 133:1). Here is the restoration of unity pictured as being as precious as the oil of priestly consecration. Jesus was anointed with the Holy Spirit so even His robes radiated with God's glory.

Brothers dwelling together in unity, is like the dew of Hermon, coming down upon the mountains of Zion; For there the Lord commanded the blessing—life forever (verse 3).

In the outer court we see the history of Israel represented. In the holy place the history of the church is represented. In the holy of holies, the coming Messianic Kingdom is represented. There we will see all that the intercessions of Christ have availed for His people. There will be the restoration of unity. "The wolf also will dwell with the lamb, the leopard shall lie down with the kid and the calf and the young lion and the fatling together; And a little boy will lead them" (Isa. 11:6).

To the over comers mentioned in the messages to the seven churches in Revelation, Jesus made the following promises.

"I will grant to eat of the tree of life, which is in the Paradise of God" (Rev. 2:7); "He ... shall not be hurt by the second death" (Rev. 2:11); "to him I will give some of the hidden manna, and I will give him a white stone and a new name written on the stone" (Rev.2:17); "to him I will give authority over the nations . . . and I will give him the morning star" (Rev.2:26,28); "and they will walk with Me in white for they are worthy , , , I will not erase his name from the book of life, and I will confess his name before my Father" and His angels. (Rev. 3:5); "I will make him a pillar in the temple of My God, . . . I will write upon him the name of My God, and the name of the city of My God, the new Jerusalem which comes down out of heaven, from My God, and My new name" (Rev. 3:12); "I will grant him to sit down with Me on My throne, as I also overcame and sat with My Father on His throne" (Rev. 3:21).

Psalm 134 presents the closing benediction.

Behold, bless the Lord all servants of the Lord who serve by night in the house of the Lord. Since the fall of Adam, the world has been a place of darkness into which a great light has come. We are the light bearers who have seen it and can lift our hands from this earthly place of darkness to the sanctuary in heaven to bless the Lord, and it is He who blesses us from Zion.

Nearness

Some Closing Remarks

On the mount of transfiguration, the Father made a brief comment after introducing His Son, saying, "listen to Him" (Mark 9:7). Though it was heard by only three of the disciples, it was recorded to benefit the entire human race. This short phrase, "listen to Him," does not present us the option of accepting one thing He said and discarding another. It does mean that by everything He said and has written, we will be judged (John 12:48). Jesus does later on ask a question. " . . . when the Son of Man comes, will He find faith on the earth?" (Luke 18:8). I think He meant faith in what He had said. Without that faith, it is impossible to please Him (Heb.11:6).

In the nearness to Jesus, the message was "listen to Him." I think it was the humility of Moses that made him such a good listener to all of God's instructions. Perhaps his appearance with Jesus on the mount was meant to illustrate that to the disciples. Elijah's presence may then well-represent the boldness the disciples would need to face all the foreign gods and idols in their up coming ministry even as Elijah had done.

God did not ask for balance of certain kinds of music or song or praise or the building of three tabernacles as Peter suggested. His balances are not like our balances, even as His thoughts are not our thoughts. I do understand the importance of praise but it's not a substitute for nearness. Let me illustrate.

It is quite common to hear people quote from Hebrews in the NKJV about boldly entering into the holy of holies. The assumption is that music will lead the way. But this text is not meant to be just a nice verse we can choose, as off a supermarket shelf, or a preferred ingredient from the book of Hebrews.

The Greek word for it is not just used in 10:19, (where it speaks of the boldness or confidence to enter) but also in three other passages. In 3:6, there is the boldness to hold fast. In 3:14, there is the boldness to draw near. In 10:35, there is the boldness not to cast away. We should ask why worship leaders quote only the one in 10:19 while they ignore the three that prepare us for entry into the holy place.

In practical experience, the *boldness to draw near* comes first. It's the first thing God seeks to do for people who have little or no regard for Him. He draws them to Himself, and He confirms His presence with His Word that convicts and His promises that delight.

Israel, as descendents of Abraham, knew they were God's people living under His promise. With the return of Moses to Egypt came God's *affirmation* of His promises in mighty signs and wonders in Egypt, the cloud and pillar of fire going before them, and the crossing of the sea on dry ground. These were a testimony to God's ability to fulfill His promises so Israel would *hold fast.*

How happily Israel sang the song of Moses. "He has cast the horse and rider into the sea." The miracle affirmed that God was good and His promises were sure. It was easy and wonderful to sing about God's wondrous power and promises.

"The Lord is my strength and song, and He has become my salvation; He is my God and I will praise Him; my Father's God and I will exalt Him."–Ex. 15:2 NKJV.

"You in Your mercy have led forth the people whom You have redeemed."–Ex.15:13 NKJV.

"You will bring them in and plant them in the mountain of Your inheritance."–Ex.15:17 NKJV.

It took only a three-day journey into the wilderness for music and song to change to grumbling. Israel was not lacking for song or music. Neither God nor Israel complained about that. What was lacking was faith in the Word God had spoken.

The millions of Israel demonstrated they *did not hold fast* to the promise and affirmation. Instead, they *cast away* God's promise, *did not boldly enter* God's provisions, and died in the wilderness because of unbelief (Heb. 3:19).

We also prefer to have our music and singing about God and His promises as a fine replacement for His provision of an enduring relationship with God that makes access into the holy place unhindered.

The first three uses of boldness are needed to establish faith. The fourth is to enjoy Him and His provisions now and forever.

It is true that as Israel journeyed from camp to camp, the tribe of Judah, meaning "may he be praised," was up front. And the Levites with trumpets of rams' horns were before the ark around Jericho. But the tribes of Dan, Asher and Naphtali formed the rear guard. By appointment they had a different position and responsibility then the other tribes. But for them all, there was equal access to God's presence and His Word spoken from the mercy seat that was camped and carried in the midst of Israel.

There was also equal representation on the breastplate and shoulder straps of the high priest. God will not violate His own instruction on favoritism (Jam. 2). He does not elevate music, which He had instructed David to position east of the altar of sacrifice, to a place of higher importance before Him than the work of intercession in the holy place at the altar of incense.

That's where "God jealously desires the Spirit which He has made to dwell in us" (Jam.4:5) to meet and intercede with Him. Sunday morning music and midweek prayer meeting attendance records illustrate what our preferences are. God's kingdom consists of all the fullness of Christ, not only our preferences.

Judah, representing praise, may have been up front in Israel's journey through the wilderness and camped by the entrance gate on the east side, but the priesthood had the privilege of nearness to God in the holy place.

David understood that when he said we should enter His gates with thanksgiving and His courts with praise. These were not places of nearness, but the way to it. David danced before the ark. But not before he had consecrated himself with burnt offerings and the peace offering of accepted nearness. He even clothed himself with the robe and ephod of a priest. The death of Uzza had brought David back to listening to God.

It appears from reading I Kings 2:28 that David brought more than just the ark to Jerusalem. The horns of the altar that Joab had taken hold of would have been the altar of sacrifice, and it would have been placed east of the tent he erected as the temporary resting place of the ark. It was David who placed the singers and musicians before (not in) the tabernacle of the tent of meeting until Solomon finished constructing the temple (I Chron. 6:38). For nearly the next thousand years of Israel's history yet to come, David instructed Solomon to place the singers and musicians east of the altar (II Chron. 5:12; I Chron. 28:11–21), a good indication of how worship will be done when Jesus returns to Zion.

David was a man who longed for a nearness to the presence of God. He was willing to take off his robes of royalty and put on the robe of a priest to humbly enthrone the King of Kings on mount Zion (Ps. 2:6). He was acting as a servant going before King Jesus.

Like the tabernacle of David, the church is also a temporary dwelling place. We also first need to learn from and listen to the tabernacle of Moses so we know how to live in the tabernacle of David and with boldness prepare to take on the governmental responsibilities of the Temple of Solomon, which represents the coming kingdom in which we will reign and rule with Christ.

We can imitate the music of David or for that matter of our culture, but not the heart of David. He had a remarkable relationship of union with his God. How prophetic and complete was his testimony of the sufferings and glories of the coming Messiah in the Psalms set to music and meant to be sung by Jew and Gentile. So if our heart is not like the heart of David, then it will need to spend time in the tabernacle of Moses. It will humble any pride and enable us to acquire a heart like David, or better still like Christ Himself.

There is an abundance of people who like a certain kind of music and for whom a particular style of music is important. Some of them might refer to the parable Jesus gave of the prodigal son, saying there was music and dancing at the repentance and return of the son. But it was the gate east of the altar that was in type. Here was the place of repentance where one by faith entered into the righteousness of Christ. This was not the holy place. For the prodigal, the party was over the following morning. The journey of a servant of God begins at the gate but is meant to lead to the holy place. The elder son was not denied the joy of celebrating, but the Father's work of establishing the kingdom to come still needed to be done. He probably had never interceded for his brother and certainly did not esteem him very highly by calling him "this son of yours."

Others may refer to the example of the last supper, where "they sang a hymn" (Matt. 26:30). When He offered His hymn of praise, it was the beginning of a whole series of events. Jesus was about to be made sin and make His life the sin offering for the world. He was, so to speak, on the way to the altar, which the offerer always approached from the east through *the gate*. When He had been made sin, He cried out, "It is finished." *The altar* had done its work. The requirements of the law were satisfied. Then He appeared to the disciples and pointed to all that the law and prophets had said, and their eyes were opened. *The Laver*, the Word of God, was doing its work. Pentecost came, and they now found themselves in the holy place as the royal priesthood of God, breaking *the bread* of His presence everywhere they went and bringing *the light* of the lampstand into the darkness of the nations. Churches were established, and *the altar of incense* became the place of prevailing prayer and intercession. The tabernacle of David was being fulfilled and realized in the church (Acts 15:16, Amos 9:11).

I'm not saying they never sang another hymn. Paul encourages them to sing when they come together. I am not opposed to music. I love singing and the harmony of peoples' voices. But music was never meant to become an easy substitute and fix for our ignorance of the fullness of Christ, presented at the altar, laver and in the holy place.

Did the early church have difficulties with this issue? Yes. And the writers of the Epistles addressed them. They did not suggest that the Psalms and hymns and songs of David should be thrown out because they were 1000 years old. They did not reason or argue that they were hard to understand, and they were for the Jews, not us Gentiles, who like our own culture and music better. Jesus did not say that upon His return He would be looking for a great musical performance. His Father did say:

"Ask of Me and I will give You the nations for Your

inheritance, and the ends of the earth for Your possession. You shall break them with a rod of iron"–Ps.2:8,9.

When Jesus returns, His word spoken from the Jerusalem throne will bring every culture, principality and dominion subject to this word.

> " . . . every knee will bow to me, and every tongue shall give praise to God."–Rom.14:11.

No culture or denomination will then be doing its own thing.

In the book of Revelation, when all the redeemed from the nations of the earth are before the throne of God, have you noticed how almost every act of worship and praise is the spoken word?

In Rev.4:8, there are four living creatures who do not cease *to say,* "Holy, Holy, Holy is the Lord God Almighty, who was, who is, and who is to come."

In Rev. 4:11 (NKJV) there are twenty-four elders *saying,* "You are worthy, O Lord, to receive glory and honor and power."

In Rev. 5:9, the four living creatures and twenty-four elders sang a new song *saying.* Were they "saying" or "singing?" We see the same thing in Rev.15:3 where "they sang the song of Moses . . . and the song of the Lamb saying." If Gods thoughts are not our thoughts, should we not ask the question of whether His thoughts on music are the same as ours?

Is it possible that the testimony of the saints is the music of heaven? Take notice how many times they *speak* the praises of God around His throne. I'll list another 9 references in Revelation: 5:12–13; 7:10,12; 11:17; 19:1,3,4,6. And yes, the 144,000 sang a new song that they alone could learn and sing (Rev. 14:3).

In the Old Testament era, they also sang a new song. Then

they sang in the outer court and on the way to it. The reason for praise was the same. The location was different. They sang because "He has done wonderful things, His right hand (of authority) and His holy arm (of obedience and conduct) have gained the victory for Him (over the earth and sin and death and hell). The Lord has made known His salvation; He has revealed His righteousness in the sight of the nations (Ps. 98:1,2). For He is coming to judge the earth" (verse 9).

It may be that the redeemed of earth will bring with them the Psalms and hymns and songs of David to sing before the throne of God. Perhaps the songs of the redeemed will restore to heaven what Lucifer destroyed with his rebellion. What is obvious to me is the abundance of "saying" the praises of God in heaven. That may not be exciting to a human mind, but it is a new song in heaven.

And what is a new song? Here is my view.

In John 16:14, Jesus is speaking of the Holy Spirit and saying that when He comes, "He shall take of mine and disclose it to you." Well, there was a Pentecost, and those who seek the Word that became flesh find that the Spirit takes of this Christ and reveals Him to them in His word.

It is a joyful privilege to have the Spirit of God take of the Son of God and reveal Him to a child of God. This child of God can then speak of this glorious Son of God in praise to the heart of God.

When sinners can speak to the Father of the glory and perfections of the Son, it is not just a new song for the sinner on earth as Stephen's testimony in Acts 7:56 illustrates, but it is also a new song in heaven never heard before by angels who long to look into this mystery (I Pet. 1:12), and it's a new song to the Father who had "a book of remembrances written before Him for those who fear the Lord; who esteem His Name and who spoke (of Him) to one another" (Malachi 3:16).

The tabernacle presents an abundance of these perfections and reasons why Jesus was the delight of the Father.

God places far greater value on His Word than man does. The record of the prophets and Jesus and the apostles would support the record of the Apostle John's vision in the book of Revelation. The testimonies of the hosts of heaven and redeemed of earth are a significant portion of the music and worship of heaven.

What the tabernacle of David foreshadowed of the coming age of the church, the vision of John foreshadows of the age to come. When Jesus came to establish the tabernacle of David, most of Israel rejected Him and His message, while multitudes of Gentiles welcomed it.

John in his vision of things to come does not emphasize singing and music at the entrance but the testimonies of those who have learned to abide in Him in the holy place, who know their God and speak His praises around the throne. The absence of this emphasis in the church is an indicator to me of how ill-prepared the church on this continent is for His second coming. The present time of deception will sort wheat from tares.

It is encouraging for me to know that in countries of significant persecution, God's written testimony is treasured and read and sought after. They will have a testimony before the throne. This continent may well have mostly excuses and statistics.

There is a great need to restore to the church a knowing of the scriptures and the Son of God that is the author of it. Our need is not unlike Paul, who writes in one of his longest sentences, "that I may know Him" (Phip. 3:8–11).

The tabernacle is a necessary foundation for a comprehensive vision and knowing of the fullness of this Christ.

TATE PUBLISHING & *Enterprises*

Tate Publishing is committed to excellence in the publishing industry. Our staff of highly trained professionals, including editors, graphic designers, and marketing personnel, work together to produce the very finest books available. The company reflects the philosophy established by the founders, based on Psalms 68:11,

"THE LORD GAVE THE WORD AND GREAT WAS THE COMPANY OF THOSE WHO PUBLISHED IT."

If you would like further information, please call
1.888.361.9473
or visit our website
www.tatepublishing.com

TATE PUBLISHING & *Enterprises*, LLC
127 E. Trade Center Terrace
Mustang, Oklahoma 73064 USA